Adobe Captivate 7
The Quick Visual Guide

Wayne Pascall

Adobe Captivate 7

The Quick Visual Guide

Copyright © 2013 by Wayne Pascall

Table of Contents

1 - New Features in Captivate 7

Captivate 7 has some new exciting features that make building eLearning projects even more powerful and interactive.

Drag and Drop Components

You can now add drag and drop interactions in Captivate 7. This has been a missing and requested feature for a long time. Now learners can use drag and drop interactions on courses published for both the PC and iPad platforms. You can choose from a variety of drag-drop combinations with variations in what a drop target can accept, reject, or replace with audio feedback.

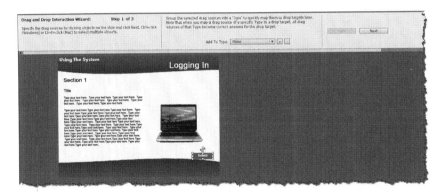

Reusable and Shared Advanced Actions

Anyone who builds advanced actions in Captivate knows how be very time consuming this task can be, often involving rebuilding the same advanced action for the same or other projects. Now you can build your advanced action just once and reuse it in the same project or others if needed. This upgrade is a welcomed time saver.

Improved 508 Compliance

Captivate 7 has improved options for accessibility and 508 compliance. You can now specify the **Tab Order** for interactive objects as well as directly import slide notes into the Accessibility panel.

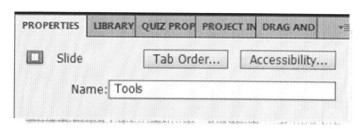

Additions to Smart Learning Interactions

There enhancements to the Smart Learning interactions of the previous version and 15 new ones. Here is a list of the new interactions.

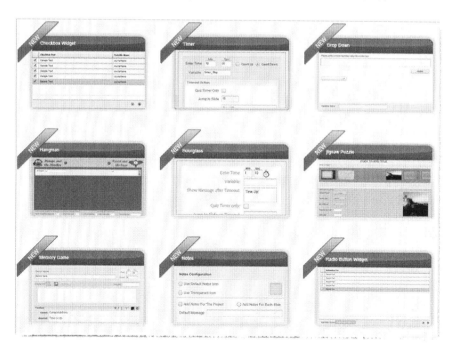

New Smart Interactions:

- *Checkbox Widget*
- *Timer*
- *Drop Down*
- *Hangman game*
- *Jeopardy game*
- *Hour Glass*
- *Jigsaw Puzzle*
- *YouTube Interaction*
- *Memory Game*
- *Notes*
- *Radio Button Widget*
- *Scrolling Text*
- *Web Object*
- *Table*
- *Image Zoom*

Improved LMS Integration

Captivate 7 promises better integration with Tin Can, SCORM and AICC compliant Learning Management Systems. This includes Moodle, Blackboard and Questionmark Perception.

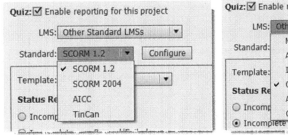 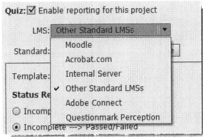

Equation Editor

The Equation Editor is a nice addition for Math, Science and Engineering courses. This addition should be appreciated more in the Academic world than the world of corporate training.

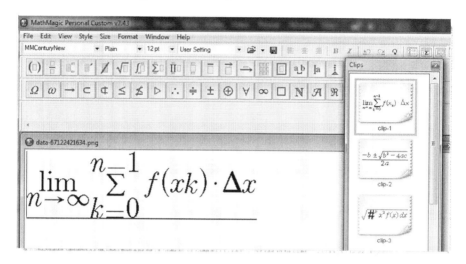

Capture System Audio with Screen Recordings

You can now capture all system sounds played on your Computer during recording. Use the system audio edit options to modify and synchronize the system audio in your project.

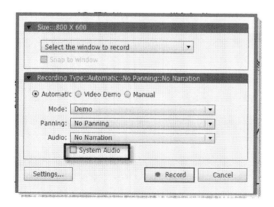

Import Questions in GIFT Format

This feature allows you to import questions in GIFT format, saving you time from tedious copy and pasting.

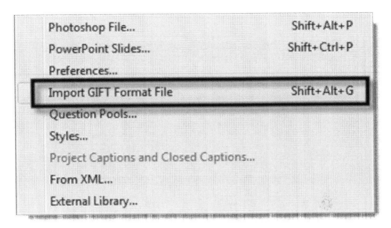

Multi-SCO Packager

The Multi-SCO Packager that was part of Captivate 5 and missing in Captivate 6 is now back in Captivate 7. It is used for combining several published SCOs into one packaged zipped file.

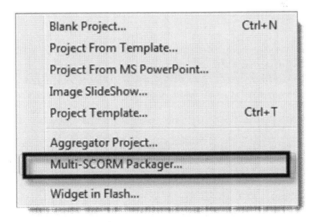

Adobe Captivate App Packager

The Adobe Captivate App Packager allows you to produce your projects as native iOS and Android applications. You can embed HTML5 animations for mobile devices using **Adobe Edge Connect** and you will need an **Adobe PhoneGap Build** service.

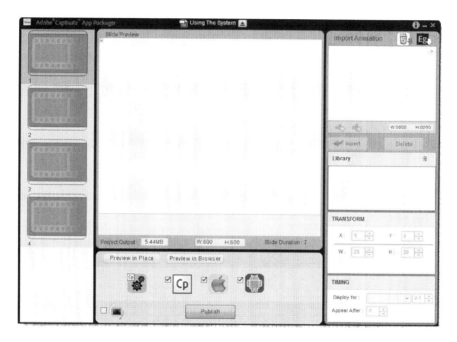

2 – Themes, Preferences, Object Styles & Master Slides

Importance of a Template

Having a style guide or template is essential for consistency in your project. I cannot overemphasize the importance of this step before you begin anything in Captive. Templates give all elements of your project a consistent and professional appearance, automates the design of new elements in your project, saving you lots of time and money from less rework. Templates will create standardized placeholders for different elements on your screens. Later, you can substitute those placeholders with your content. I highly recommend that your first step should be establishing how you want your project to look (size, color of elements, fonts, media etc.) then building templates around those specifications and have every designer in your project build their work from the templates.

Templates are especially important for very complex projects with several designers on a team, some of whom may be working remotely. When working on eLearning projects with many teams or with a huge design team, it is critical to balance creativity with consistency. Even if you are working alone on an eLearning project, with the flexibility to be creative, you should first decide on the details of how you want the course to look, and then build a template around those specifications. This template will be your style guide throughout the entire project. Since styles and tastes are subjective, if you leave it up to each designer in a team to choose what they want, you could end with an eLearning course with several different sizes of fonts for headings, different colors for the background, text captions designed differently for the same course and much more inconsistency. You would save yourself wasted efforts in rework and heartache later in your project, if you build your own templates.

Using Templates

If you decide to build your own templates, you will need to establish what your preferences are, save them as a template, and then reload the template to begin your project.

Captivate 7, has four features that developers can use to build templates:

1. **Themes**
2. **Master Slides and Master Slide Layouts**
3. **Placeholders**
4. **Object Styles**

Later in this chapter, we will work through an exercise where we will use a combination of themes, master slides, master slide layouts, placeholders and object styles to build a template.

Using Themes

The Themes feature is new in Captivate 7 and is similar to the themes in PowerPoint. They are pre-built templates. They blend backgrounds, styles, fonts, and layouts and give a quick consistent design to your project just by selecting one. If you do not have the time to build a template scratch then selecting a theme or customizing one is the answer.

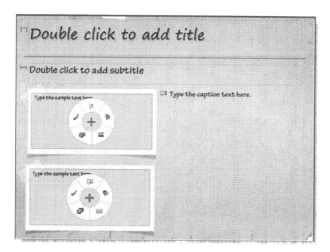

Pre-built Themes

Captivate 7 is loaded with a variety of 10 themes:

- Black and White
- Black
- Blackboard
- Blank
- Clean Blue
- Clouds
- Green
- Timeworn
- White
- Woody

Creating Your Own Themes

You can create your own themes or customize existing ones, save them for reuse in other projects. Themes are very powerful ways of quickly applying visual design to a Captivate project with just **one click**.

To create a new theme:

1. Load one of the preset themes by clicking one on the Themes bar.

2. Ensure that the Master Slide panel is open (**Window > Master Slide**). Click the Master Slide tab to navigate to the master slide view.

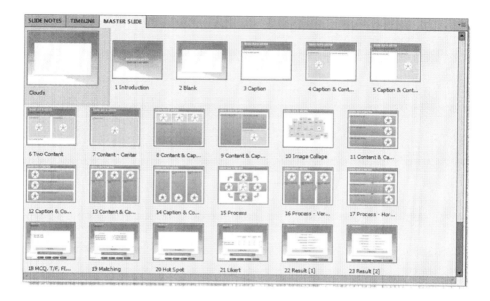

3. Click the parent master slide

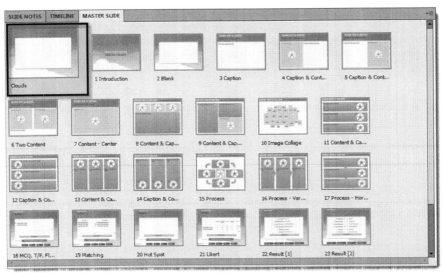

4. In the Property Inspector, click the "Clear" icon that looks like a trash can (Note this will not delete the theme).

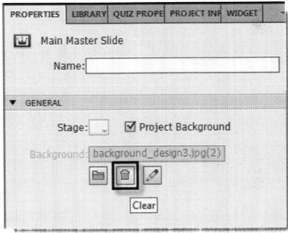

5. Delete any remaining objects from the master slide.

The **parent** master slide now becomes blank.

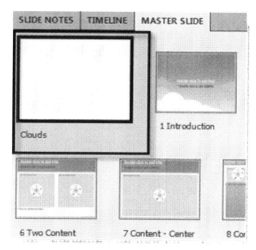

6. On the parent master slide, either load a new graphic as your background or design your own.

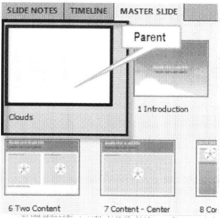

7. In the "Background" field, click the browse folder icon to load an image for your new background

OR on the blank Parent master slide, create your own design using Captivate tools.

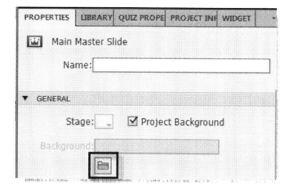

8. On the Children Master slides, ensure that **"Use Master Slide Background"** and **"Show Main Master Slide Objects"** are checked.

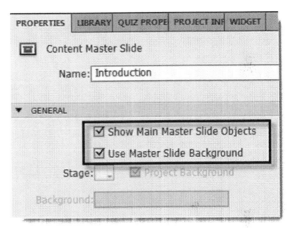

9. The **children** layout slides will INHERIT your design from the **parent** master slide

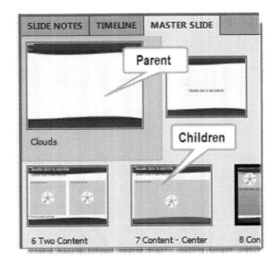

10. Save your design as a theme. **Themes > Save Theme As.**

Save your theme in a location and name that you can easily access. Captivate 7 saves the theme with a **.cptm** file extension. The default location of Captivate themes is:

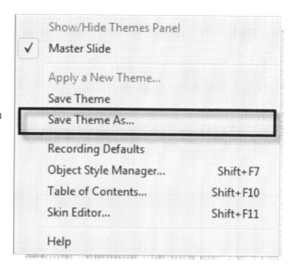

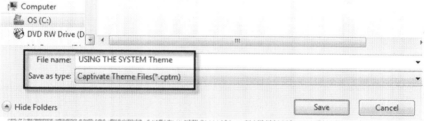

11. Click out of the Master Slide panel – Filmstrip, then click the Show Themes panel icon at the top control panel. Your new theme populates the collection of themes at the top.

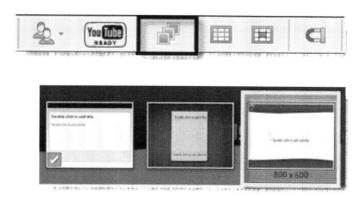

12. To set your new theme as the default theme, right – click the thumbnail for your new theme and select "**Set as Default Theme**."

13. You can also load themes from your collection by clicking the **Browse** button on the top right section of the Themes bar.

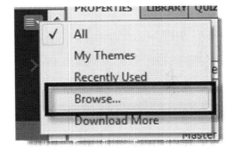

Using Master Slides

Master slides in Captivate 7 function similar to master slides in PowerPoint. Changes in the master slide will be reflected in all the slides linked to it – a huge time saver. You can also have more than one master slide linked to different dependent slides. Master slides are great for background graphics and objects that remain consistent throughout the project.

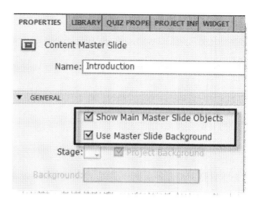

Master slides in Captivate 7 are designed a little differently than previous versions. They are actually improved with different layouts for different kinds of content. Master slides in Captivate 7 are linked to Themes. The master slides will adopt the visual design of the selected theme. The purpose of master slides is to reduce rework and achieve more efficiency and consistency. Just like Power-Point, Master slides in Captivate 7 are divided into 2 main sections. There is the main or parent master slide and the content or children master slides. The children master slides usually inherit the characteristics of the parent master slide when **"Use Master Slide Background"** and **"Show Main Master Slide Objects"** are checked.

Master slides are however, limited in controlling the styles of objects that may vary from screen to screen. Object styles complement master slides in these kinds of variations. A little later we will learn how to use Object Styles.

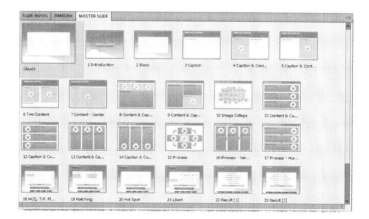

To use Master slides:

1. Select a **theme,** by clicking one from the Themes bar.

2. Right click on any slide in the Filmstrip and choose:

Slide > New Slide From
And choose the Master slide to which you want to link. Each Theme has at least 23 different variations of master slides linked to it.

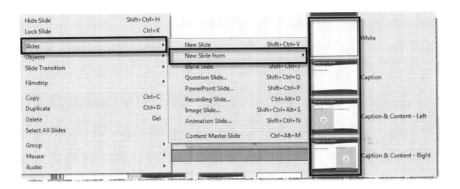

The Clouds Theme for example has the following master slides. Make a choice depending on your content:

Content Master Slides:

- **Introduction**
- **Blank**
- **Caption**
- **Caption & Content – Left**
- **Caption & Content – Right**
- **Image Collage**

- Content & Caption – Horizontal
- Content & Caption – Vertical
- Caption & Content – Horizontal
- Caption & Content – Vertical
- Process
- Process – Vertical
- Process – Horizontal

Quiz Master Slides:

- MCQ, T/F, FIB, Sequence
- Matching
- Hot Spot
- Likert
- Result 1
- Result 2

3. Add objects to your master slide that will remain consistent throughout the project. Some examples are:

Background graphics, navigation buttons, borders, H1 headings. Do **not** add objects that will change from slide to slide.

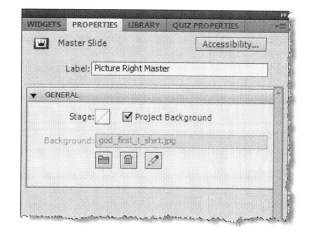

4. Master slides can be renamed, edited, duplicated, copied and pasted.

The fastest way build a new master slide is by **duplicating** an existing one, then renaming it and modifying it.

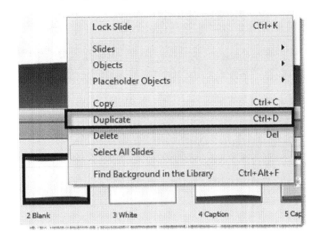

Using Placeholders in Master Slides

A Placeholder acts as a temporary container for content. Placeholders are great for designing the general look of your template. You may decide you want text on the left and images on the right on certain screens. Insert a placeholder for each kind of content acts as a temporary guide until you are ready to add content.

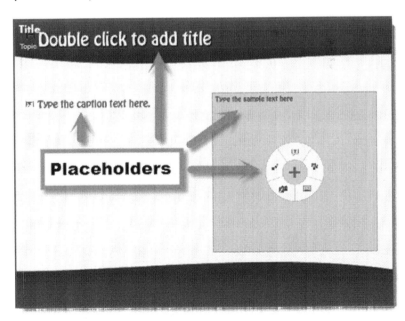

Inserting Placeholders

1. To insert a placeholder object in a master slide, **right-click** the master slide and select **Placeholder Objects,** then choose the type of placeholder from the menu: **Text Caption, Sub-Title, Rollover Caption, Image, Rollover Image, Animation, Text Animation, Video Object, Smart Shape** and **Content Placeholder.**

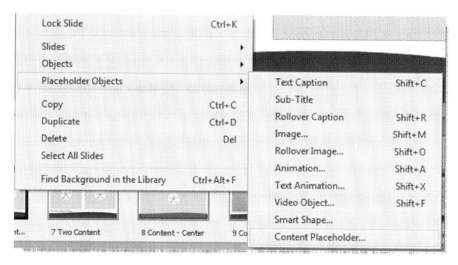

2. Choose **Content Placeholder** if you are unsure of the kind of content you want to add. This adds a **Placeholder Wheel** with interactive sections for adding a: **Caption, Text Animation, Image, Video Object** and **Animation.**

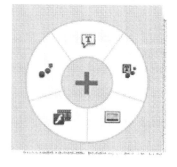

3. Position the placeholder in the desired location on the master slide.

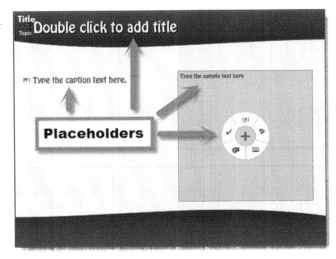

Characteristics of Placeholders Objects

- Placeholder Objects are temporary containers for content that will be added later. They are ideal for templates.
- Placeholder Objects can be added **only to master slides**. Placeholders added to master slides display in the Filmstrip slides that are linked to them.
- Add content to Placeholder Objects by double-clicking them
- Placeholder Objects have the prefix "**Placeholder**" in their names located in the properties panel.

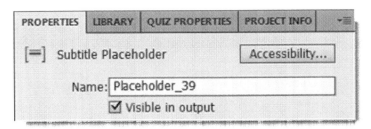

- Placeholder Objects **cannot be seen** when the project is **previewed** or **published**. This remains so until actual content is substituted.

Adding Content to Placeholders

1. If you are in the master slide view, **exit out master slide view** by clicking the filmstrip.

2. Add content to a placeholder, by simply **double-clicking it** on the stage.

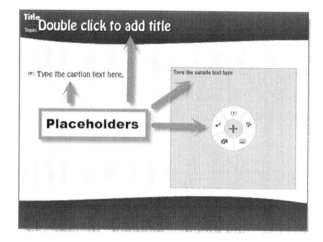

Using Object Styles

Object styles in Captivate are similar to the styles feature of the other Adobe products like Dreamweaver, PhotoShop, and Illustrator. Styles of objects can be saved as presets and reloaded when needed. If for example, you have decided that all H1 headings at the top of each screen should be in Arial font, size 28, then you can save this as a style with a name of your choice and loaded when each time you create an H1 heading. This not only results in shorter development time, but in more consistency. Time is money. A savings in time is a savings in money.

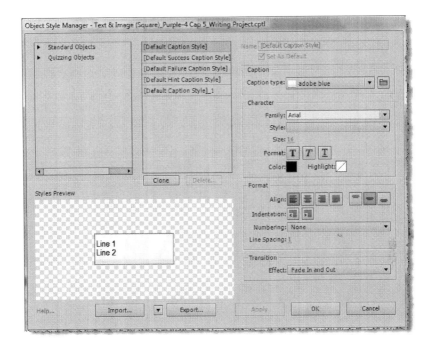

Building Your Own Object Styles

1. From the **Themes** menu select **Object Style Manager.**

2. Expand the two categories of objects (**Standard Objects** and **Quizzing Objects**) and select from the lists, the object whose style you want to edit.

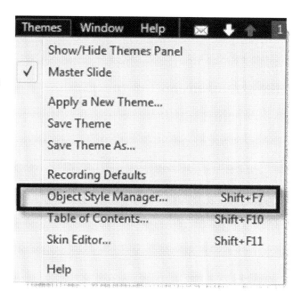

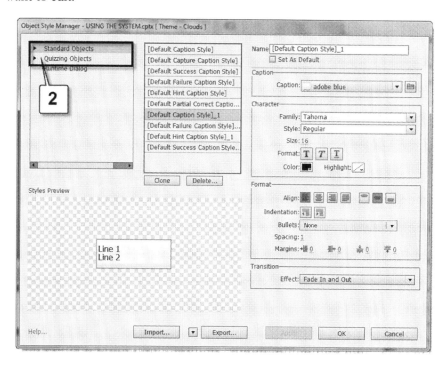

3. For your desired object, select from the list of available styles.

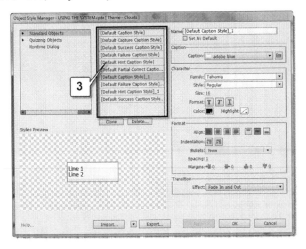

4. You can also create your own style. In this example, we will be defining a style for a **Highlight Box**

From the list of styles, select one that is closest to the new style you want to create.

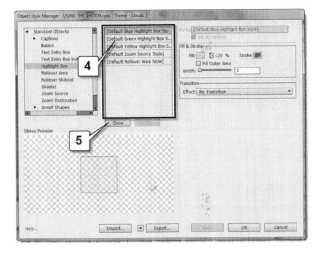

5. Click **Clone.**

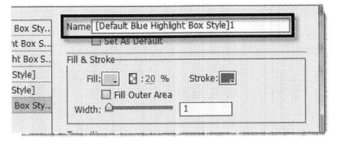

6. Enter a name of your choice for the new style you want to create.

7. Select a color for the **Fill** and **Stroke** of the **Highlight Box.**

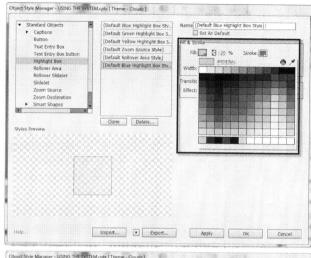

8. Click **OK.**

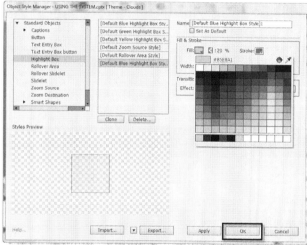

Note:

From the Object Style Manager, you can define styles for:

Standard Objects:

- Captions
  - o Text Caption
  - o Rollover Caption
  - o Success Caption
  - o Failure Caption
  - o Hint Caption
- Buttons
- Text Entry Boxes
- Highlight Boxes
- Rollover Areas
- Rollover Slidelets
- Zoom Source and Destination
- Smart Shapes
  - o Smart Shape
  - o Title
  - o Subtitle
  - o Rollover Smart Shape
- Buttons
  - o Skip Button
  - o Back Button
  - o Continue Button
  - o Submit Button
  - o Clear Button
  - o Review Button
  - o Retake Button
- Progress Indicator
- Review Area

Quizzing Objects:

- Captions
- Correct Caption
- Incorrect Caption
- Retry Caption
- Timeout Caption
- Incomplete Caption
- Advanced Feedback Caption
- Title (Question/Result)
- Question Text
- Answers/FIB Text
- Header (Matching/Likert)
- Matching Entries
- Likert Question
- Scoring Result
- Scoring Result Panel
- Hot Spots

Components of Templates

To create powerful templates in Captivate 7, use a combination of

- Themes
- Master slides
- Placeholders
- Object Styles

As mentioned before, this will not only significantly reduce your development time but also allow you to achieve more consistency in your Captivate 7 projects. The new features in Captivate 7 such as themes and master slide layouts offer opportunities for creating stronger templates than previous versions.

Saving Templates

1. To save your project as a template, click **File > Save As**

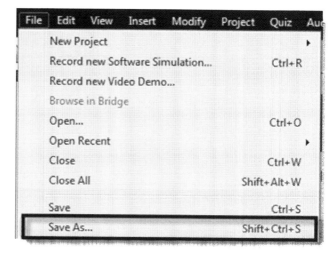

2. In the **Save As** drop-down menu, choose **Captivate Template Files (*.cptl)**.

Note:
Captivate projects have file extensions with **(.cptx)** while templates have a **(.cptl)** extension.

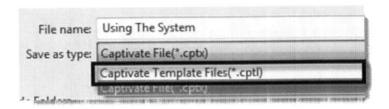

Applying Templates

1. To continue editing a Captivate template double-click the file with the extension (.cptl)

The procedure for applying your template settings to a new project is different. Double-clicking a **(.cptl)** file will **not** load a (.cptx) project file; instead this action simply launches your template file for further editing.

2. To begin a new project from the template you have created so that the project adopts all the settings of your template:

Click **New Project > Project From Template**

3. OR from Captivate's **welcome screen** select **From Template**.

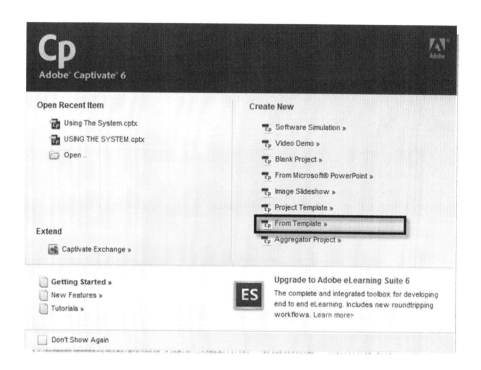

4. Navigate to where your template file is saved and select it.

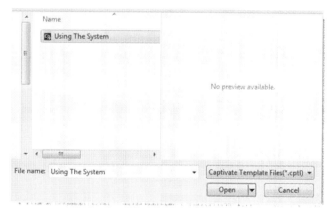

5. Your project is loaded with an **untitled1.cptx** name and all the characteristics of your template. Save it under a name of your choice with the **.cptx** extension

3 - Recording

One of the powerful features of Captivate is that it allows you to record any activity on a screen or portion of a screen. Captivate will automatically add text captions, click boxes and text entry boxes depending on the recording mode chosen.

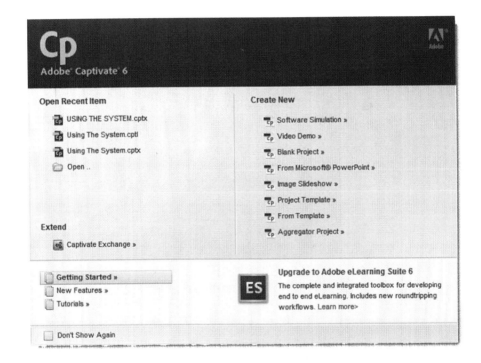

Recording Modes

1. Using the **Automatic** Record feature will automatically create screen captures every time the mouse is clicked.

2. Captivate has four capture modes: **Demo** (Demonstration), **Assessment** (Assessment Simulation), **Training** (Training Simulation) and **Custom**.

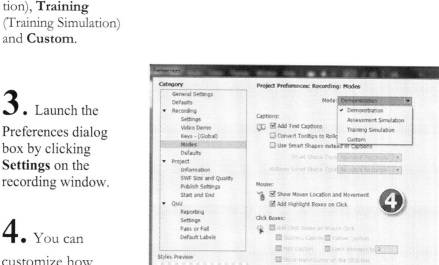

3. Launch the Preferences dialog box by clicking **Settings** on the recording window.

4. You can customize how Captivate behaves in each **Mode** by tweaking the settings in the **Preferences** dialog box under **Recording >Modes**.

Demonstration Mode

The demonstration mode is useful when you want to simply demonstrate a procedure or feature in an application. The disadvantage of recordings in this mode is that it does not allow much user interaction. The user passively views the movie as it plays.

When recording in the demonstration mode, Adobe Captivate:

- *Adds text captions using labels of the clicked portions of the application.*
- *Adds highlight boxes to areas of the recording where mouse clicks were performed.*
- *Adds text where text was typed manually during the recording.*

Training Simulation Mode

The training mode is useful when you want the user to experience a simulation of a procedure or using an application. This mode lets the user interact with the content in some way. After correctly performing an action, the user is taken to the next slide.

When recording slides in training simulation mode, Adobe Captivate:

- *Adds click boxes at places where the user is required to click the mouse.*
- *Adds text entry boxes for text fields requiring user input. Failure and hint captions are added to each text entry box.*

Assessment Simulation mode

The assessment mode is useful when you want to test how well the user has understood a procedure. This kind of assessment goes beyond the interaction needed in a quiz. Rather than merely selecting correcting answers, the user must for example click on the right sections of an application and in the proper in order. In Kirkpatrick's model of evaluation, this will be a true level 3 evaluation. You can set a score for every correct click. You can also set the number of times the user can attempt a procedure.

When recording slides in assessment simulation mode, Adobe Captivate:

- *Adds click boxes at places where the user is required to click the mouse.*
- *Adds text entry boxes for text fields requiring user input. Failure and hint captions are added to each text entry box.*

Custom Mode

The custom mode is useful on a project where you need a mix of features available in the other modes. This mode allows you to fully customize the way Adobe Captivate behaves when recording. Using the custom mode, you can create a project that is part demo, part training simulation, and part assessment. No Adobe Captivate objects are added by default during recording in the Custom mode. You need to specify how you want Captivate to function when recording in this mode.

Preparing to Record

Before beginning a recording in Captivate you should have the following established

1. Recording Settings and Mode

Determine beforehand you want your recordings as a demonstration or a simulation where users must interact with sections of the screen to proceed. Use the **Recording Settings** and **Object Style Manager** to specify the dimensions of the recording (e.g. 1024 x 768), what object objects will be added automatically to your recordings and the color and properties of these objects. Captivate 7 has a new feature where you can add Smart Shapes in place of Captions. Determine whether you want to use features like this.

2. A Script or Storyboard that outlines the steps

Have a script that outlines the steps you must take to perform your recording. This should be concise and not cluttered with extra information. If these steps are in a storyboard you may need to summarize into a simplified version such as:

1. *Click the Home Button*
2. *Click the My Tasks tab*
3. *Click the Edit Icon...*

3. A trial run of the steps

Conduct a practice recording session before your actual recording. In this way you can determine if you encounter any obstacles that need to be addressed before performing your actual recordings.

4. Clean system that is to be recorded

Ensure that the screens you will capture in the recording are free of clutter and any items that will distract your users. Extra toolbars in browsers should be closed. If you are recording steps in a system, ensure that the system is ready, that the right names of people, buttons and other parts of the interface are in place. This will save you the time of having to mask over things after recording. Know beforehand whether there is proprietary information like customer names and account numbers that will need to be masked or blurred in the recordings.

Creating a New Recording

1. To begin a recording project, click **Software Simulation** on the welcome screen.

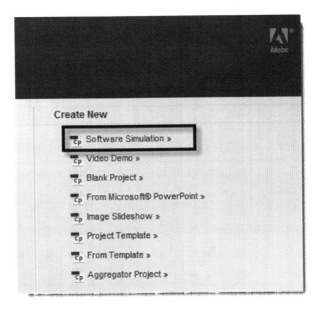

2. Select whether you will record an **Application** or **Screen Area.** Choose whether to include **System Audio.** This is a **new feature** in Captivte 7.

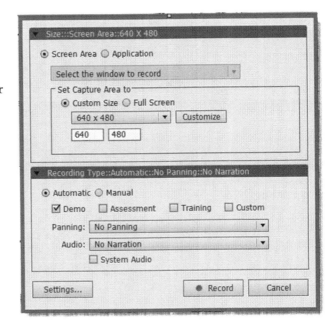

3. If you selected **Application**, choose which one from the **Select Window** drop down box.

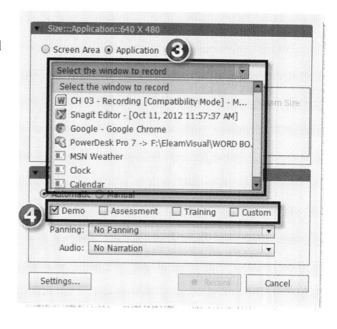

4. Choose your **Recording Type**:
A) **Demo, Assessment, Training**, or **Custom**

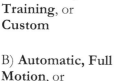

B) **Automatic, Full Motion**, or **Manual.**

5. If you select **Screen Area**, choose your **dimension** from the drop down box or custom your own **width and height** of the recording.

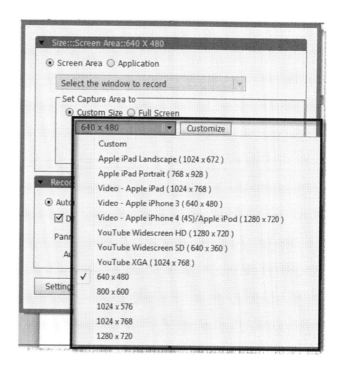

6. You can also begin a new recording project from **inside Captivate** by clicking on:

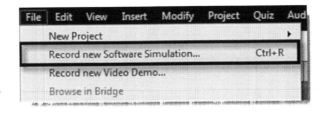

File > Record new Software Simulation.

This will load the recording window, where you can select your recording options.

7. You can also begin a new recording from **inside Captivate** by clicking on:

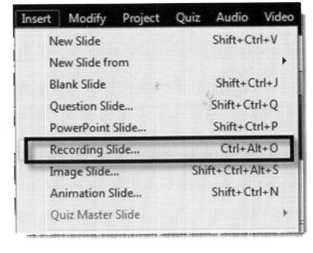

Insert > Recording Slide.

OR

from inside Captivate, click the **Record** button on the top toolbar.

8. Select where you want to place the new recorded slides.

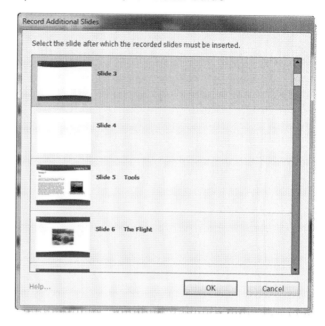

9. Select the **window** you want to begin capturing and choose your **Recording Type** and options including **Mode**, **Panning** and **Audio**.

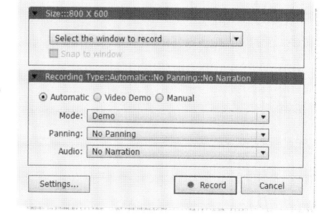

10. Enable **Panning** if you would like Captivate to capture areas of the screen beyond the recording area when that occurs. If not, leave this drop-down menu to the default setting of **No Panning**.

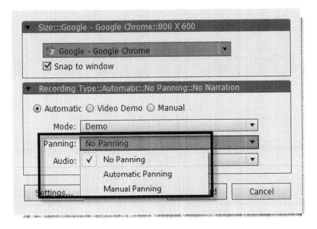

11. Drag the red box to the area that you want to record and ensure that **Snap to Window** is checked.

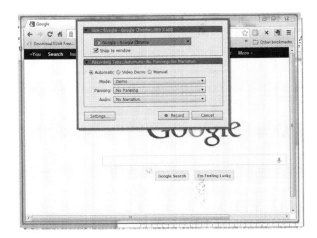

12. Click **Record** and click the areas of the screen according to your script.

Enabling the camera sound in Captivate for each time you click helps you know when Captivate has captured a screenshot.

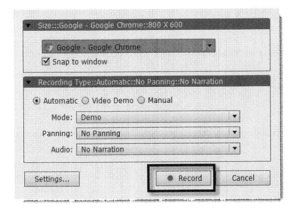

13. Enabling the **Camera Sounds** in Captivate will play a helpful camera shutter sound each time you perform a click action in recordings. This lets you know when Captivate has captured a screenshot.

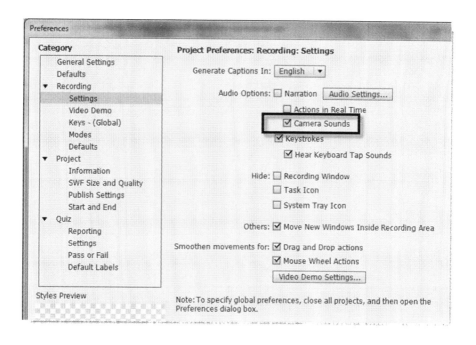

14. To **stop** the recording, press the **Esc** key or click the Captivate task icon on the system tray.

Recording a High Definition Full Motion Video

High definition full motion video recording is a new feature in Captivate 7. Full Motion recording was in previous versions but not in high definition. In simulation and demonstration recording modes, Captivate captures a **series of screen shots or images**. In these modes, Captivate captures images **only upon mouse clicks**. In Full Motion video mode, Captivate captures a real non-editable **video file** of everything that moves on the screen, from the time the record button is pressed. This mode can be helpful for complex actions on the screen like demonstrating how to draw and paint in artist applications. Animations, videos and **anything that plays and moves on the screen** are also captured; hence the name Full Motion Video as opposed to a series of images. Captivate puts a small video icon on all screens captured in the video mode.

To record a Full Motion Video in High Definition, simply select the **Video Demo** mode.

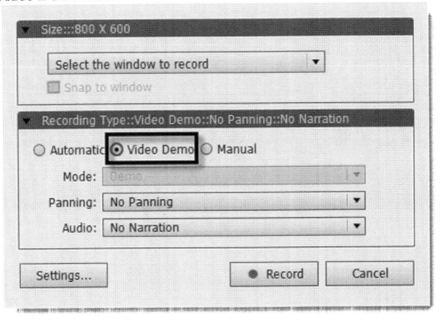

4 - Adding Text Captions

1. To insert a text caption: On the **Object Toolbar**, Click the Caption tool.

Or from the **Insert** menu: Click: **Standard Objects > Text Caption.**

2. Under the **General** tab, Choose the Caption design.

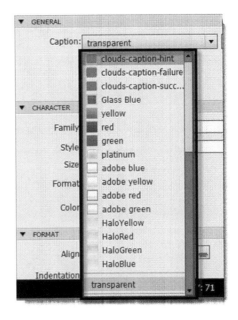

Tip

You can design your own captions in Photoshop, save them in the same directory where the other Captivate captions are located (C:\Program Files\Adobe\Adobe Captivate 7 x64\Gallery\Captions), then click the **folder icon** under the **General** tab to load them.

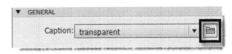

53

3. Enter your text in the Caption

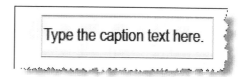

4. From the Property Inspector, Under the **Character** Tab, select the attributes of your Text Caption such as Font: **Family, Style, Size, Format** (Bold, Italic, Underlined, SuperScript, SubScript) and **Color**.

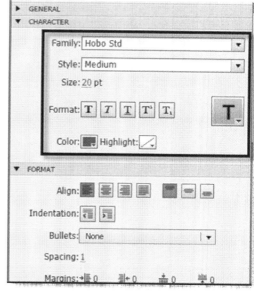

5. From the Property Inspector, Under the **Format** Tab select the attributes of your Text Caption such as: **Align** (Left, Center, Right, Justified), Indentation, Type of **Bullets** (New), **Line Spacing** and **Margins** (New). Margins create a space around the outer perimeters of the text.

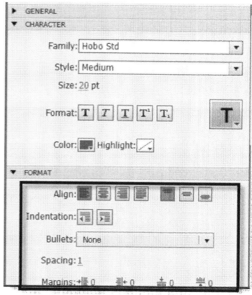

6. To convert your text to a bullet style, first click the caption, the under the **Format** tab, select a style of bullets from the **Bullets** drop-down menu.

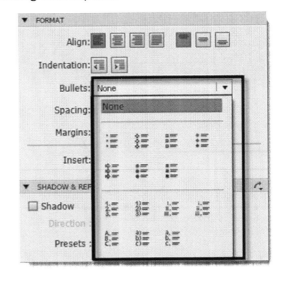

7. Double-click the **Margins** (Left, Right, Top, Bottom) values to change them.

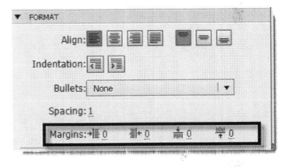

8. Select other characteristics of your text such as: **Shadow, Reflection** (New), **Timing, Transition, Audio** if any and **Transform**.

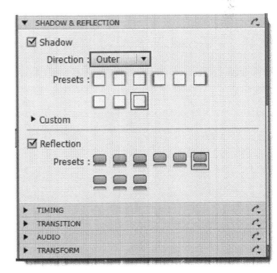

9. To add **3D Text Effects**, click the **Text Effects** Icon (T) in the **Character** panel of the Property Inspector and choose one of the presets.

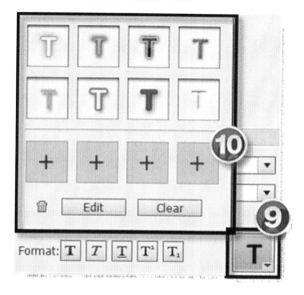

10. Click the **plus (+)** buttons to add and configure your own effects.

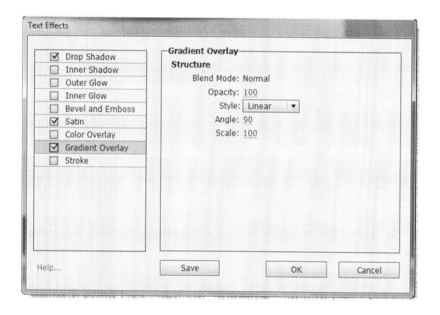

5- Adding Visuals

Adding Images

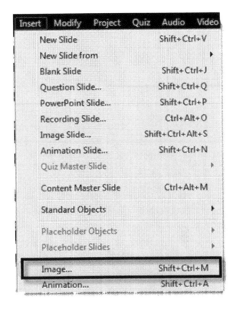

1. To insert an image: Click on:

Insert / Image.

2. Choose your image from the **"Open"** window.

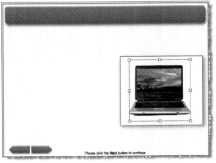

3. The image appears on the screen. Move your image to the desired position.

Editing Images

1. To **change the order** of your image in relation to other objects on the screen, right click on the image and choose from:

- *Bring to Front*
- *Send to Back*
- *Bring Forward*
- *Send Backward*

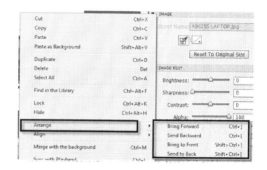

2. The **image's order** in relation to other objects is represented here in the timeline. You can also click and drag objects here upwards or downwards to change their order.

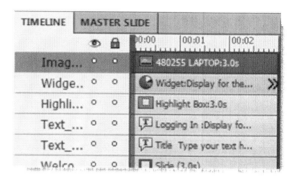

3. In the **Properties** panel, choose the properties of your **Image:**

Shadow & Reflection, Timing, Transition, Position, Size

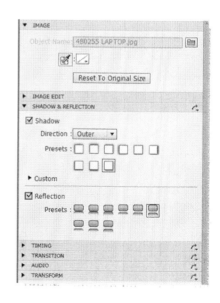

4. Using the **Image Edit** panel under the **Properties** Inspector, you can further edit an Image's:

Brightness, Sharpness, Contrast, Alpha, Hue, Saturation, Color Inversion, Grey Scale

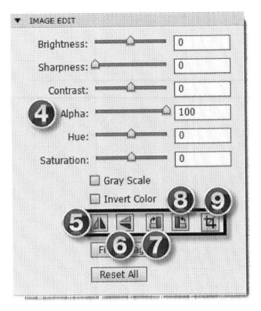

5. *Flip Image Horizontal.*

6. *Flip Image Vertical.*

7. *Rotate Right.*

8. *Rotate Left.*

9. *Crop.*

You can change an image's **transparency** *by manipulating its* **Alpha** *value:*

- *100% Alpha – The image is opaque*
- *0% Alpha – The image is completely transparent*

Adding Character Images

Character images are a new feature in Captivate 7 that allow you to add different personas to your courses. The characters are divided into four categories: **Business**, **Casual**, **Illustrated** and **Medicine**. They can act as avatars, agents, guides thus adding a personal touch to your content and enhance learning.

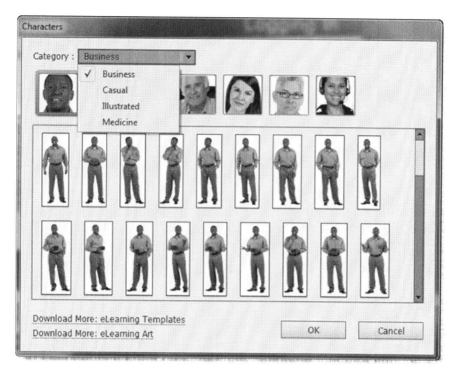

1. In To insert a **Character image** in your project, click **Insert > Characters**

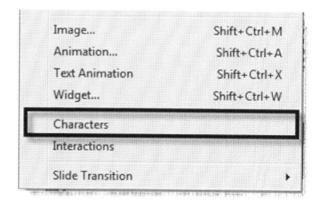

2. There are four categories of characters: Business,
Casual, Illustrated and
Medicine. Each category has
different characters in
different poses.

Click the **Category** drop-
down button:

 a. *Select a* **Category**
 b. *Select a* **Character**
 c. *Select a* **Posture**

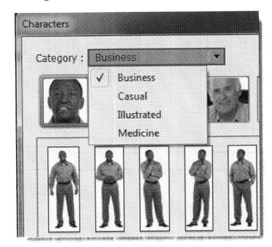

3. Position your character in the desired location on the stage.

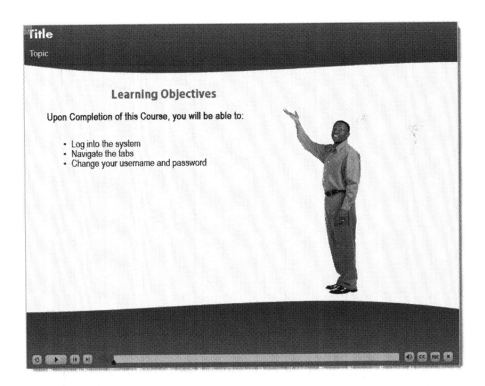

Adding Smart Shapes

Smart Shapes are a new feature in Captivate 7. They are similar to the shapes you find in PowerPoint which means you can add a lot of visually appealing graphics right inside of Captivate without relying on external software like PowerPoint.

1. In To insert a **Smart Shape** in your project, click **Insert > Standard Objects > Smart Shape**

OR

Simply Click the **Smart Shape** tool on the tool bar and select the shape of your choice.

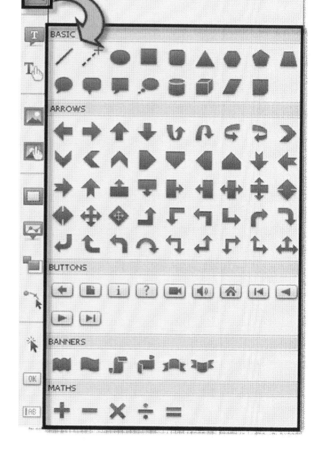

2. Click and drag your cursor on the stage to draw the shape you have chosen.

Adding Equations (New)

You can now create and edit mathematical equations in Captivate 7. The editor launches MathMagic, a multi-purpose equation editor, formula editor, and scientific symbol editor.

1. To add an equation to your project, Click **Insert** > **Equation**. A default equation is inserted and **MathMagic** opens

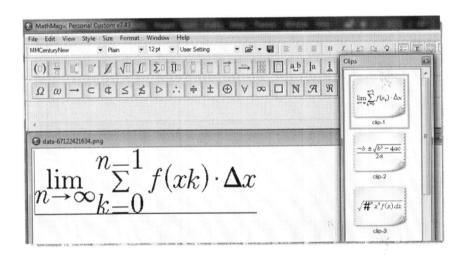

2. **Edit** the equation as desired and click **Save** and **Close**. The changes will be reflected on the Captvate slide.

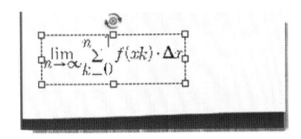

3. To edit, **double-click** the equation on the screen, make your changes in the MathMagic application. Click **Save** and **Close**. Use the link below to find out more about **MathMagic**: http://www.mathmagic.com/

6- Adding Interactivity

Interactivity encourages users to interact or do something with your lesson instead of passively viewing it. When users are encouraged to interact with various sections of the lesson, not only will they remember it better, but also they would be more motivated to complete it. Several pages of digital content without any interaction from the reader can quickly become boring. Good instructional design practice is to have some form of interaction for every 3 to 5 screens of content. Following this rule will ensure that your modules are not mere "page turners." Here are some ways Captivate 7 allows you to add interactivity to eLearning content:

- Buttons
- Click Boxes
- Rollover Captions
- Rollover Images
- Rollover Slidelets
- Text Entry Boxes
- Variables, Scripts and Widgets
- "Check Your Knowledge" Questions
- Games (Inserted as a Flash animation)
- Widgets
- Hyperlinks
- Learning Interactions
- Drag and Drop Interactions (New)

Buttons

You can use five types of buttons in Captivate 7:

- Image buttons
- Text buttons
- Transparent buttons
- Widget buttons
- Smart Shapes as Perpetual Buttons

Image buttons are conveniently pre-built buttons from the Captivate library with labels such as "Next" and "Forward." **Text buttons** allow you to use your own text to label buttons. **Transparent buttons** allow you to customize the transparency of your button or even make it invisible. **Widget buttons** are conveniently pre-built flash buttons that can be accessed from the Captivate widget panel. Smart Shapes are a new feature in Captivate. You can also configure a Smart Shape to function as a button. When used on master slides, **Smart Shape buttons** function as perpetual buttons, displaying on every slide linked to them.

Adding Buttons

1. To insert a **Button**: On the **Object Toolbar**, Click the Button tool.

Or, from the **Insert** menu: Click: **Standard Objects > Button.**

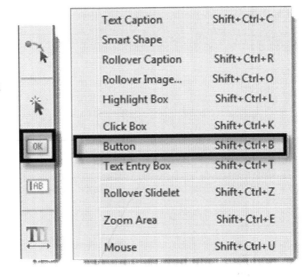

2. Position your button on the screen.

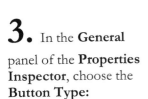

3. In the **General** panel of the **Properties Inspector,** choose the **Button Type:**

- *Text Button*
- *Transparent Button*
- *Image Button*

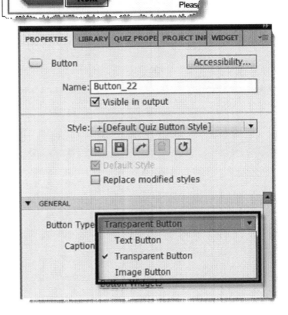

4. For **Image Buttons** you can select from the available styles

Or

5. You can browse your computer for your own image buttons by clicking here.

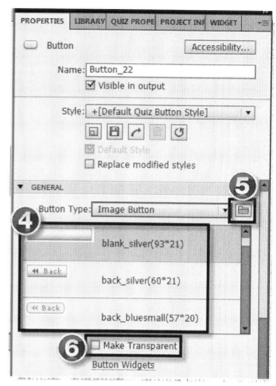

6. Check the **Make Transparent** check box to make the button transparent.

7. In the **Action** panel of the Properties Inspector, from the **On Success** drop-down menu, select the action you would like your button to perform after successfully clicking on it.

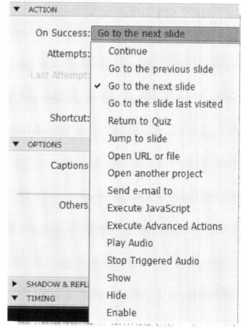

Brief Description of Button Actions

Continue
The user is taken to the next defined action after clicking button.
Go To Previous Slide The user is taken to the previous slide after clicking button.
Go To Next Slide The user is taken to the next slide after clicking button.
Go To Last Visited Slide
The user is taken to the previously viewed slide after clicking button.
Return to Quiz
The user is taken back to the last attempted question if it was answered incorrectly.
Return to Quiz
The user is taken back to the last attempted question if it was answered incorrectly.
Jump To Slide The user is taken to the specified slide after clicking button.
Open URL Or File
After clicking button, the user is taken to a website or file which opens.
Open another project
After clicking button, the user is taken to the specified Adobe Captivate project.
Send e-mail To
After clicking button, the user is taken to the default e-mail editor, which opens with an e-mail draft, addressed to the recipient as specified.
Execute JavaScript
After the user clicks button, Adobe Captivate executes the specified JavaScript.
Execute Shared Action (New), re-uses a shared Advanced Action
Execute Advanced Actions
After the user clicks button, Adobe Captivate runs the specified script. This includes multiple actions that are performed in the order specified by the user.
Play Audio, A user-click triggers a specified audio file to play
Stop Triggered Audio
After the user clicks the last triggered audio file stops playing
Show
After the user clicks button, the specified hidden object is made visible.
Hide
After the user clicks button, the specified object becomes hidden.
Enable
After the user clicks button, another object in the project is activated.
Disable
After the user clicks button, another object in the project is disabled.
Assign
After the user clicks button, the value of the specified variable is set inside the object.
Increment
After user clicks button, the value of the specified variable is increased accordingly.
Decrement
After user clicks button, the value of the specified variable is decreased accordingly.
Apply Effect
After the user performs an action, it triggers an effect associated with the object
No Action
When the user clicks button, nothing happens.

Using Smart Shapes as Perpetual Buttons

By adding one instance of a Smart Shape used as a button on a Master Slide, you can have navigation buttons automatically appear on every page linked to that Master Slide – a huge time saver. In the example below, we will use a Smart Shape as a **Next button** that navigates the user to the next screen on every slide.

1. To use a Smart Shape as a button, ensure that the Master Slide tab is open by clicking **Window > Master Slide**

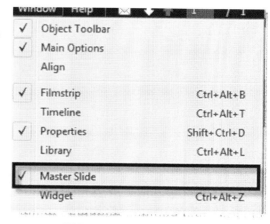

2. In the Master Slide view, click **Insert > Standard Objects > Smart Shape**

OR

Simply Click the **Smart Shape** tool on the tool bar and select the shape of your choice.

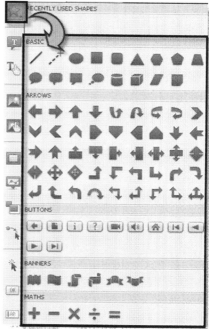

3. Click and drag

your cursor on the stage to draw the shape you have chosen. Position the Smart Shape in the desired location.

4. Double-click the

Smart Shape and **add text** for the button.

5. With the Smart Shape

still selected, in the **Properties Panel**, ensure that the checkbox for **Use as Button** is checked.

6. Under the Action

accordion, select **Go to the next slide**.

7. Under the Options

accordion ensure that **Hand Cursor** and **Pause project until user clicks** are checked.

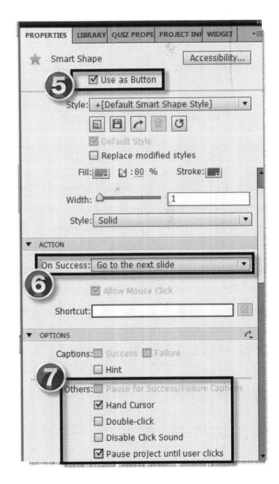

8. The **Smart Shape button** appears on every slide that is linked to the Master Slide containing it.

Click Boxes

Click Boxes function like "hot spots" that you can place anywhere, which when clicked on, performs some action like opening a web page.

1. To insert a **Click Box**: On the **Object Toolbar**, Click the Click Box tool.

Or, from the **Insert** menu: Click: **Standard Objects > Click Box.**

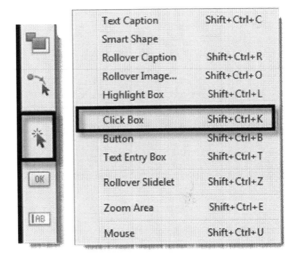

2. Select the **Options** for your Click Box.

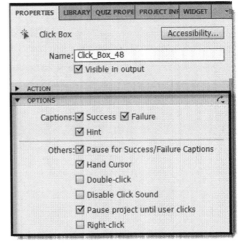

To guide the user in a simulation, insert **Failure and Hint captions** with Click Boxes. Interactions in simulations can also be scored and become part of an assessment or they can be used as mere practice exercises.

3. In the **Action** panel of the Properties Inspector, select the action you would like your Click Box to perform after successfully clicking on it.

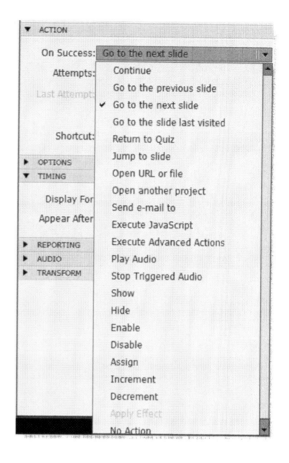

Brief Description of Click Box Actions

Continue
The user is taken to the next defined action after clicking button.
Go To Previous Slide The user is taken to the previous slide after clicking button.
Go To Next Slide The user is taken to the next slide after clicking button.
Go To Last Visited Slide
The user is taken to the previously viewed slide after clicking button.
Return to Quiz
The user is taken back to the last attempted question if it was answered incorrectly.
Return to Quiz
The user is taken back to the last attempted question if it was answered incorrectly.
Jump To Slide The user is taken to the specified slide after clicking button.
Open URL Or File
After clicking button, the user is taken to a website or file which opens.
Open another project
After clicking button, the user is taken to the specified Adobe Captivate project.
Send e-mail To
After clicking button, the user is taken to the default e-mail editor, which opens with an e-mail draft, addressed to the recipient as specified.
Execute JavaScript
After the user clicks button, Adobe Captivate executes the specified JavaScript.
Execute Shared Action (New), re-uses a shared Advanced Action
Execute Advanced Actions
After the user clicks button, Adobe Captivate runs the specified script. This includes multiple actions that are performed in the order specified by the user.
Play Audio, A user-click triggers a specified audio file to play
Stop Triggered Audio
After the user clicks the last triggered audio file stops playing
Show
After the user clicks button, the specified hidden object is made visible.
Hide
After the user clicks button, the specified object becomes hidden.
Enable
After the user clicks button, another object in the project is activated.
Disable
After the user clicks button, another object in the project is disabled.
Assign
After the user clicks button, the value of the specified variable is set inside the object.
Increment
After user clicks button, the value of the specified variable is increased accordingly.
Decrement
After user clicks button, the value of the specified variable is decreased accordingly.
Apply Effect
After the user performs an action, it triggers an effect associated with the object
No Action
When the user clicks button, nothing happens.

Examples of How to Effectively Use of Click Boxes

1. To encourage more user participation in the training versus passive learning.

2. To simulate applications and allow the user to interact with the material as they would in a real-world situation. You can have the user simulate the actual procedure of using a feature in an application. Combinations of **Click Boxes** and **Text Entry Boxes** offer very creative possibilities for building high interactivity into eLearning modules.

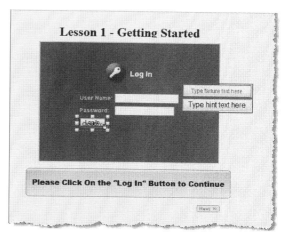

3. To give users opportunities to practice what they just learned.

4. To enable branching to other slides.

5. As links:

    1)   to websites for resources and to explore a topic further.
    2)   to other slides in branching scenarios
    3)   to open files in resources links e.g. pdf files.

6. To execute advanced actions as part of a complex interaction.

7. To trigger an effect as part of a complex interaction

Text Entry Boxes

1. To insert a **Text Entry Box**: On the **Object Toolbar**, Click the Text Entry Box tool.

Or, from the **Insert** menu: Click: **Standard Objects > Text Entry Box.**

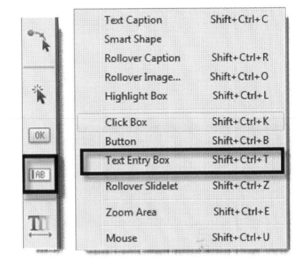

2. Choose your options under **General** tab. If you would like the user's entries to be validated for accuracy, ensure that **Validate User Input** is checked.

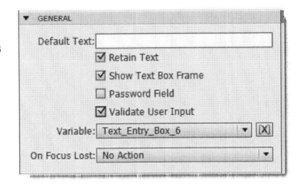

3. Click the plus sign (**+**) and Type the **Correct Entries** for the Text Entry Box.

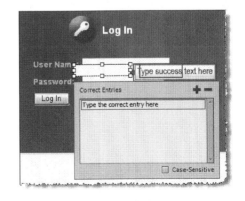

4. Choose the
actions for correct and
incorrect entries
entered by the user.

5. Select the **Options,**
Timing, Transition, Fill
& Stroke and **Position &**
Size for the **Text Entry**
Box.

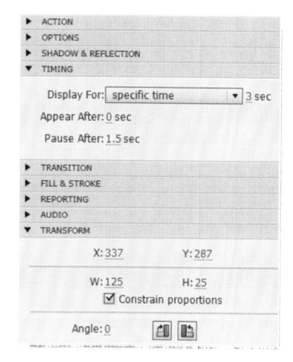

6. Choose the **Report-**
ing options for the Text
Entry Box. Choose
whether you want these
interactions reported to an
LMS and be part of an
assessment.

To activate the **Include in**
Quiz option (if it is greyed
off), ensure that **Validate**
User Input is checked
under the General tab.

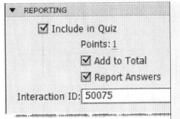

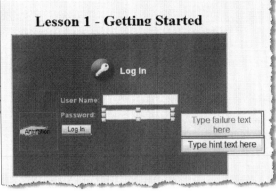

7. Type your desired **failure** and **hint** texts.

8. Add **Text Captions** that will guide the user on what action is required of them.

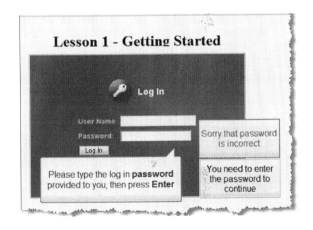

9. A Text Entry Box at run time.

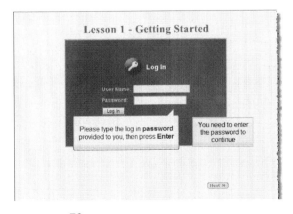

Rollover Captions

Rollover captions are convenient ways of adding information and interactivity to your modules without the screens becoming cluttered with information. You can have the user roll their mouse over a particular spot to display more information about a subject.

1. To insert a
Rollover Caption: On
the **Object Toolbar**,
Click the Rollover
Caption tool.

Or, from the **Insert**
menu: Click:
**Standard Objects >
Rollover Caption.**

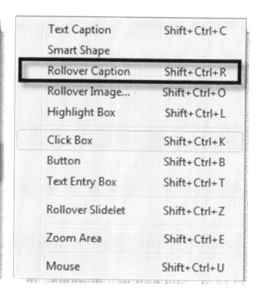

Text Caption	Shift+Ctrl+C
Smart Shape	
Rollover Caption	Shift+Ctrl+R
Rollover Image...	Shift+Ctrl+O
Highlight Box	Shift+Ctrl+L
Click Box	Shift+Ctrl+K
Button	Shift+Ctrl+B
Text Entry Box	Shift+Ctrl+T
Rollover Slidelet	Shift+Ctrl+Z
Zoom Area	Shift+Ctrl+E
Mouse	Shift+Ctrl+U

2. Type the **caption**
that the user will see
when they move their
mouse over the rollover
area.

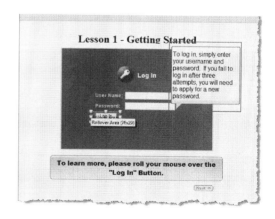

3. Select the style of caption from the **Caption type** drop down menu.

From the Property Inspector, select other attributes of the Rollover Caption such as: Font style (**Charac-ter**), Justification (**Format**), **Transition**, **Audio** (If any), **Position and Size**.

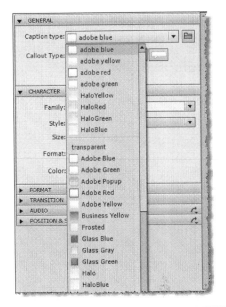

4. Position and resize the **rollover area** (the "hot spot" that triggers the caption when the mouse rolls over it).

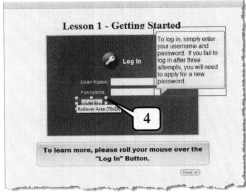

5. Add any **text caption** necessary to guide the user where they should move the mouse to activate the rollover caption.

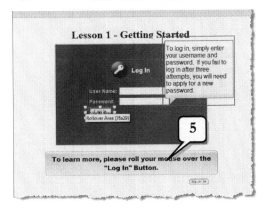

Rollover Images

Rollover images are convenient ways of adding visuals and interactivity to your modules without the screens becoming cluttered with information. You can have the user roll their mouse over a particular spot or text to display a related graphic about a subject.

1. To insert a Rollover Image, click Insert / Standard Objects / **Rollover Image.**

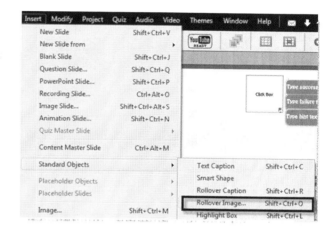

2. Navigate to where your **image** is located and select it.

3. Position and resize the **rollover area** (the "hot spot" that triggers the image when the mouse rolls over it).

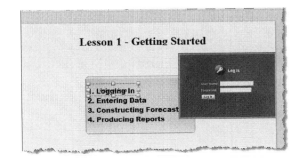

4. Add any **text** necessary to guide the user where they should move the mouse to activate the rollover image.

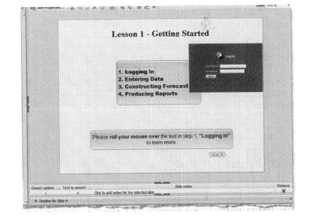

Rollover Slidelets

Rollover Slidelets are powerful ways of adding information and interactivity to your modules without the screens becoming cluttered with information. They allow users of your content to access **images, text, audio and video** via one mouse rollover. Like the caption and image rollovers, the information is displayed when a user rolls the mouse over a specified spot on the screen.

1. To insert a **Text Entry Box**: On the **Object Toolbar**, Click the Text Entry Box tool.

Or, from the **Insert** menu: Click: **Standard Objects > Text Entry Box.**

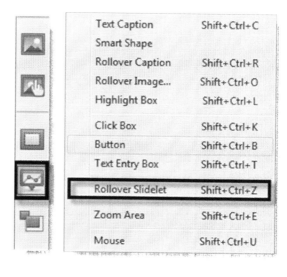

2. Choose the **border color, border, transparency, transition effect** and other attributes of the Rollover slidelet (the "hot spot" that triggers the slidelet when the mouse rolls over it).

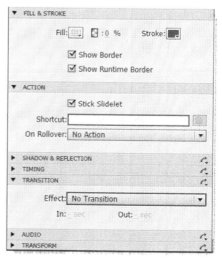

84

3. Set the position and size of the **Rollover Slidelet** and **Slidelet**.

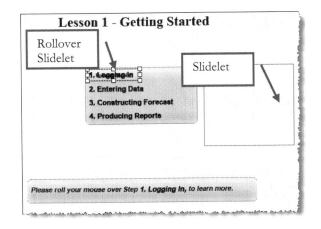

4. Select the **Slidelet** by clicking on it.

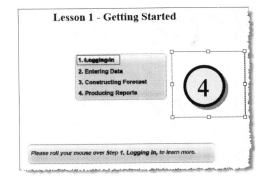

5. Using the **Insert** menu, insert contents of **Slidelet** (Image, text, video and audio). The Slidelet as well as its contents can be resized and position anywhere.

6. Add any text necessary to guide the user where they should move the mouse to activate the Rollover Slidelet.

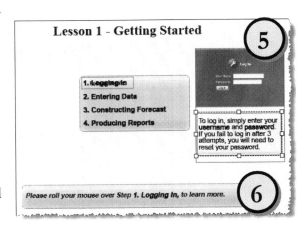

7. A **Rollover Slidelet** in action. The user rolls the mouse over "1. Logging In".

8. The image and text of the **Slidelet** appear simultaneously on the right.

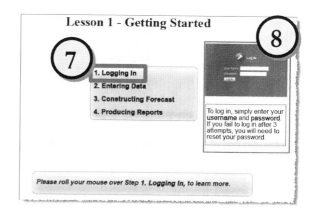

The Slidelet has its own timeline. You can adjust the timing of the Slidelet's objects (Image, text, video and audio) inside its timeline. Simply click on a Slidelet to access its timeline.

Widgets

Widgets are convenient flash objects that quickly add interactivity to a Captivate project. There are static, interactive and question widgets. Widgets are SWF files with their own ActionScript. They can be easily dragged into the captivate screen from the widget panel and their parameters configured. You can view the collection of widgets by clicking on: **Window > Widget**.

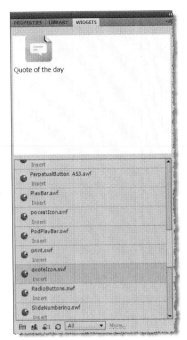

A Chart Widget prepared in Captivate 7

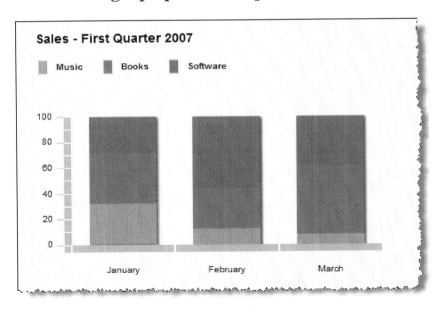

Captivate Widgets Library

- CertificateWidget
- Chart
- PerpetualButton
- PodPlayBar
- helpIcon
- print
- quoteIcon
- SlideNumbering
- TextArea
- volumeControl
- ChartsWidget
- TableWidget
- Other Widgets
- ArrowWidget
- AskanExpert
- browser
- Button
- CheckBoxes
- combobox
- MCQ
- MountainBluePlayBar
- Dropdown
- Timer
- emailIcon
- GotoSlide
- ListBox
- MacStylePlayBar
- PlayBar
- podcastIcon
- RadioButtons
- videoIcon
- VividTextCaption
- FlashButton
- NextButton

Creating New Widgets

You can also develop your own widgets for Captivate using Adobe Flash.
To develop your widget click: **File > New > Widget in Flash.**

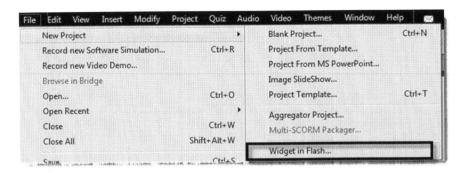

Using Widgets – The Certificate Widget

We will now look at an example of using and editing one of the Captivate 7 widgets to meet our training needs. We will use a **Certificate widget** and configure it, so that a student at the end of a training module and collects a certificate of completion with the student's name printed on it.

1. To Insert the Certificate Widget, bring the widget panel into view by clicking:

Window / Widget.

Click the **Insert** link for the "**CertificateWidget.**"

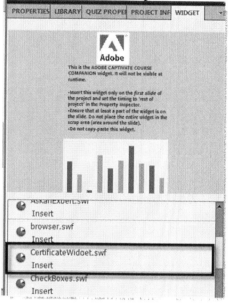

2. The **Widget Properties** window launches. Choose a Certificate **Template**

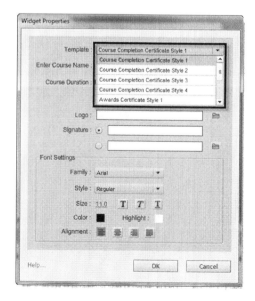

3. Enter other properties of the Widget, such as:

- *Course Name*
- *Corse Duration*
- *Logo*
- *Signature*
- *Font Settings*

4. Click **OK.**

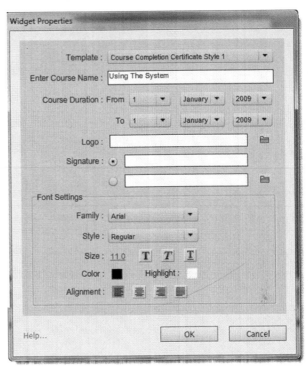

5. The **Certificate of Completion** appears on the stage.

6. The certificate at runtime is preceded by a screen that collects the user's name.

After clicking **Submit**, the user collects the **Certificate of Course Completion** with the user's name, course name, and date printed. The user can click on the Print icon to print the certificate if desired.

All Captivate widgets have their own FLA files which you can access at the path:

C:\Program Files\Adobe\Adobe Captivate 7\Gallery\Widgets \Source

Developers can **customize these widgets** by loading the (**.fla**) file in Flash, then saving it under a new file name.

Variables

Variables function as placeholders for data. The data is stored in text captions and will be displayed wherever the caption is placed. The data contained in variables can provide one or more of the following:

- Provide feedback
- Create advanced actions
- Configure widgets

System variables are contained in Captivate. **User-defined variables** are defined by the developer. Variables can be further divided into six categories.

System Variables:

- Movie Control Variables
- Movie Information Variables
- Movie Meta Data Variables
- System Information Variables
- Quizzing Variables

User Variables:

- Created by the Captivate developer

Some Useful Captivate Variables

Variable	Returns	Sample values	Description (if available)
cpInfoCurrentDateString	string	7/10/2009	Returns the calendar date in mm/dd/yyyy format using the client's system clock.
cpInfoCurrentMinutes	string	45	Returns the current minute using the client's system clock.
cpInfoCurrentSlide	number	12	cpInfoCurrentSlide uses 1-based indexing, so slide 1 of the project will return 1. Returns (rdinfoCurrentSlide + 1);
cpInfoCurrentSlideLabel	string	Logging In	Returns the label of the slide, if available.
cpInfoCurrentTime	string	19:59:27	Returns the current time in HH:MM:SS format using the client's system clock. Note: uses 24-hour clock. Returns (now.getHours() + ":" + now.getMinutes() + ":" + now.getSeconds());
cpInfoElapsedTimeMS	number	1537	Returns the amount of time (in milliseconds) that has elapsed since the movie began playing. Returns (cpInfoEpochMS – movie.m_StartTime)

Hyperlinks

Hyperlinks are a new and welcomed feature in Captivate 7. You can add interactivity to a project by hyperlinking text or drawing objects to launch web pages, navigate to certain slides and execute advanced actions.

1. To hyperlink a text or drawing object, first **select the text or drawing object.**

2. Expand the **Format** accordion in the Property Inspector and click the **Hyperlink tool.**

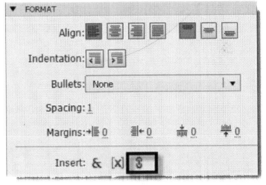

3. In the first drop-down menu of the dialog box that launches, select the **type of hyperlink** you want to create from the available options.

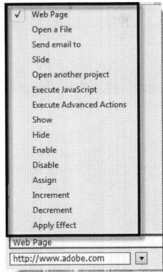

4. In the second drop-down menu, enter the text for the link if it is a Web Page and select one of the options for the type of hyperlink you chose. For a Web Page, **New** launches the page in a new window while **Current** launches the Web Page in the current window being viewed.

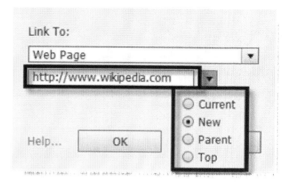

5. Click **OK**.

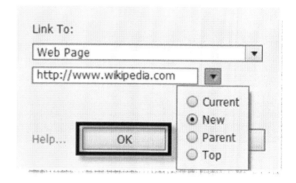

6. The text is now hyperlinked.

Learning Interactions (New)

Smart interactions allow developers to add interactivity to a project by adding widgets that encourage users click on sections of the screen to explore learning instead of passively viewing the material. There enhancements to the Smart Learning interactions of the previous version and 15 new ones. Here is a list of the **new interactions**.

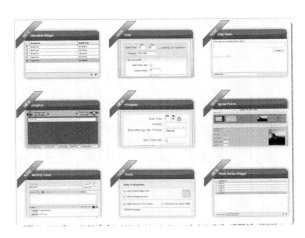

New Smart Interactions:
- *Checkbox Widget*
- *Timer*
- *Drop Down*
- *Hangman game*
- *Jeopardy game*
- *Hour Glass*
- *Jigsaw Puzzle*
- *YouTube Interaction*
- *Memory Game*
- *Notes*
- *Radio Button Widget*
- *Scrolling Text*
- *Web Object*
- *Table*
- *Image Zoom*

Let us insert and configure the **Timeline Interaction**

1. To insert a Smart Learning interaction, click **Insert > Interactions**.

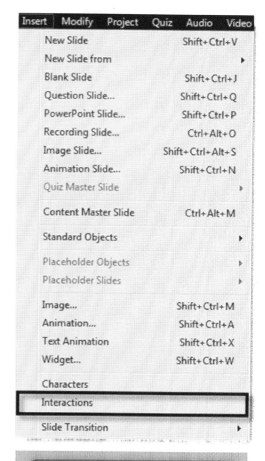

2. Choose one of the available 10 interactions by clicking it. In this case, we have selected the **Time-Line** interaction.

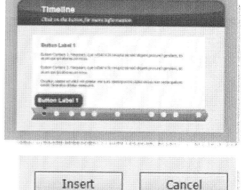

3. Click **Insert**.

4. Choose a **theme** from the list of available themes.

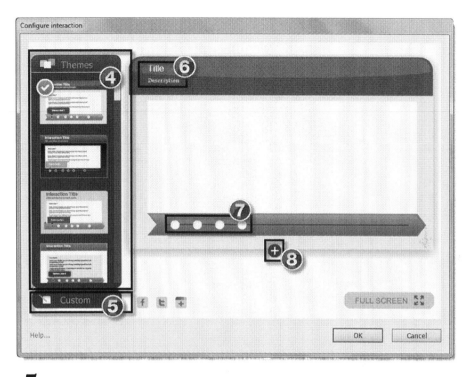

5. Click **Custom** to customize a theme of your choice or just use the available themes.

6. Double-click the **Title** and **Description** to add your own text for these fields.

7. Double-click each **button** to add your own text for its label.

8. Click the **(+)** sign to add event buttons.

9. To **remove an event button**, double-click it and click the **(-)** sign.

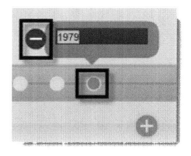

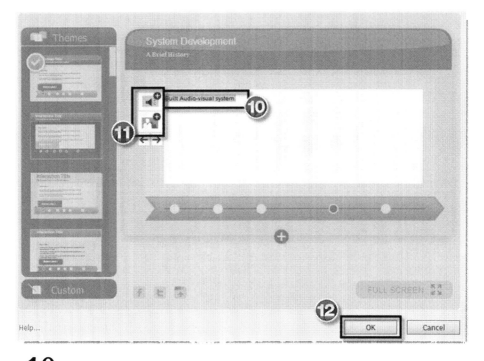

10. With each event button selected, double-click the **content section** to add **text** for that event.

11. With each event button selected, double-click the **content section** to add **audio and images** for that event.

12. Click **OK** when you are finished configuring the **Learning Interaction**.

13. Resize and position the Learning Interaction in the desired location on the stage.

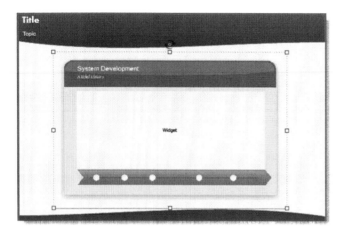

14. The Timeline Learning Interaction at runtime.

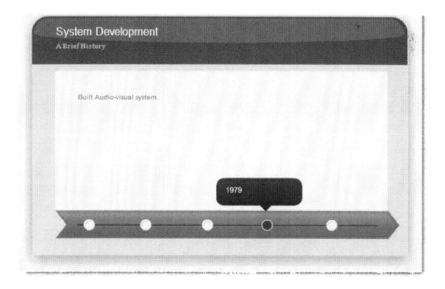

Adding Drag and Drop Interactions (New)

Using The Wizard

You can now add drag and drop interactions in Captivate 7using two methods: The Wizard and the Property Inspector. First, let's look at using the wizard method.

1. Navigate to the slide on which you want the interaction and click

Insert > Launch Drag and Drop Interaction Wizard.

2. Follow the Wizard's instructions to choose a **sources** and **targets** for the interaction and click **Next**.

Drag and Drop Interaction Wizard:	Step 1 of 3

Specify the drag sources by clicking objects on the slide and click Next. Ctrl+click (Windows) or Cmd+click (Mac) to select multiple objects.

Drag and Drop Interaction Wizard:	Step 2 of 3

Specify the drop targets by clicking objects on the slide and click Next. Ctrl+click (Windows) or Cmd+click (Mac) to select multiple objects.

3. Map the **souces** and **targets** to establish the correct answers and click **Finish**.

Drag and Drop Interaction Wizard: **Step 3 of 3**

Specify correct answers by mapping drag sources to correct drop targets. To do so, click and drag the handle at the center of drag sources.

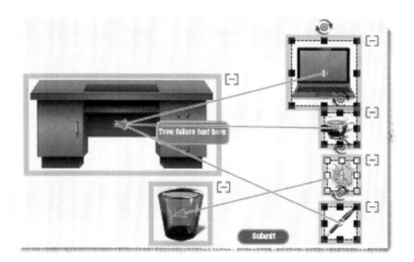

4. The Drag and Drop **Property Inspector** appears after you click **Finish**. From here, you can customize and further edit your Drag and Drop interaction with Snap Behaviors, Interaction Points, Types, Audio, Effects and Actions.

Using The Property Inspector

1. Navigate to the slide on which you want the interaction and add your source and target objects.

2. Bring the Drag and Drop panel into view by clicking Window > Drag and Drop.

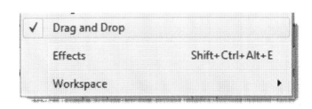

3. Click the Create New Interaction icon positioned at the top Property Inspector.

4. Now let's specify the Drag sources. Click each object that you would like to be draggable and select the **Drag Source** radio button under the **General** tab.

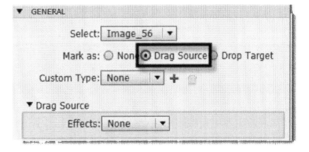

5. Apply any **Effects** to the source objects if needed.

6. Now let's specify the Drop Targets. Click each object that you would like to be a Drop Target and select the **Drag Target** radio button under the **General** tab.

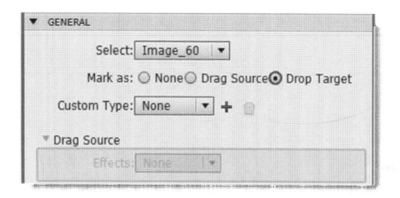

7. **Map** the **souces** and **targets** to establish the correct connections. **Click** the **drag source** and a '+' symbol will appear at the center of the drag source. Click and drag the '+' symbol and **point the arrow** to the correct drop target.

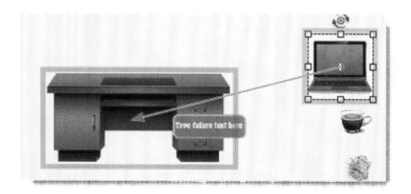

8. Using the settings under the **Drop Target** accordion, configure the options for **Accept**, **Snap Behavior**, **Captions**, **Effects** and **Audio** for the Drop Target.

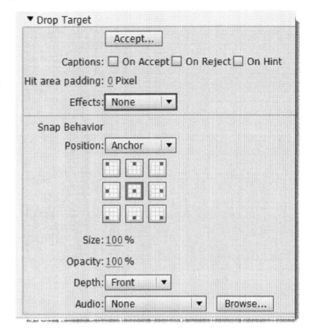

7- Adding Emphasis & Attracting Attention

Zoom Areas

1. To insert a **Zoom Area**: On the **Object Toolbar**, Click the **Insert Zoom Area** tool.

Or, from the **Insert** menu: Click: **Standard Objects > Zoom Area**

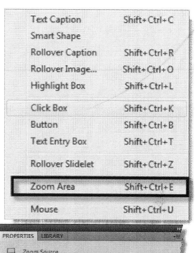

Text Caption	Shift+Ctrl+C
Smart Shape	
Rollover Caption	Shift+Ctrl+R
Rollover Image...	Shift+Ctrl+O
Highlight Box	Shift+Ctrl+L
Click Box	Shift+Ctrl+K
Button	Shift+Ctrl+B
Text Entry Box	Shift+Ctrl+T
Rollover Slidelet	Shift+Ctrl+Z
Zoom Area	Shift+Ctrl+E
Mouse	Shift+Ctrl+U

2. For the Zoom **Source** and **Destination**, select the Fill color, Stroke color, Stroke Width, transpar-

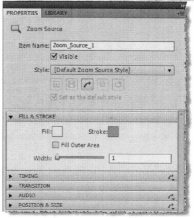

3. Adjust the size and position of the Zoom Area.

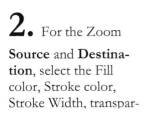

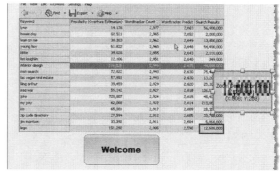

Highlight Boxes

1. To insert a **Highlight Box**: On the **Object Toolbar**, Click the **Insert Highlight Box** tool.

Or, from the **Insert** menu: Click: **Standard Objects > Highlight Box**

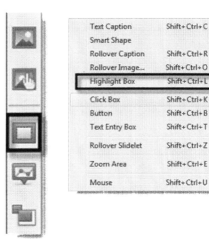

2. For the Highlight Box, select the Fill color, Stroke color, Stroke Width, transparency and other attributes.

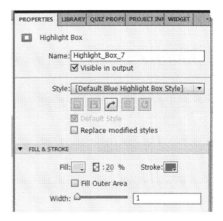

3. Adjust the size and position of the Highlight Box.

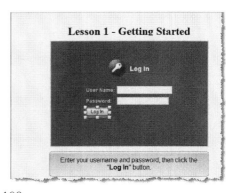

Animations

Flash Animations

1. To insert a Flash
Animation, click

Insert > Animation

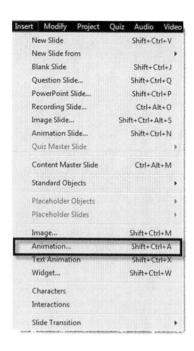

2. Navigate to where
your Flash Animation is
located.

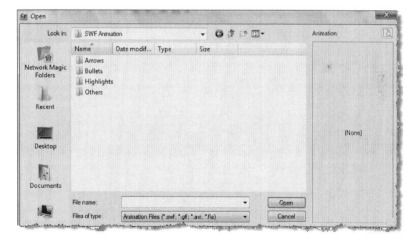

3. You can also use animations from a wide variety in the **gallery**
of Captivate 7. Go to: **Program Files/Adobe/Adobe Captivate
7/Gallery/SWF Animation**

The SWF animations are organized in **four** categories:

- Arrows
- Bullets
- Highlights
- Others

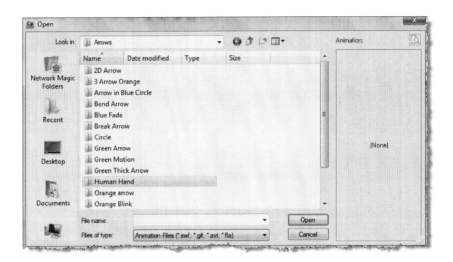

4. Navigate to your desired Flash Animation in Captivate's gallery.

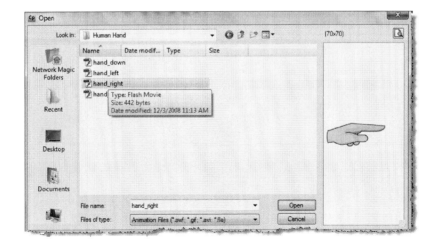

5. Select the **transition effect, timing** and **other attributes** of the animation.

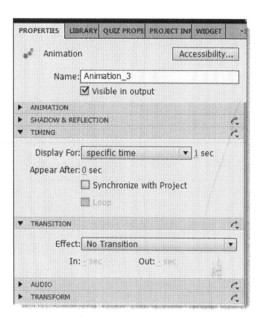

6. Set the desired position and size of your animation.

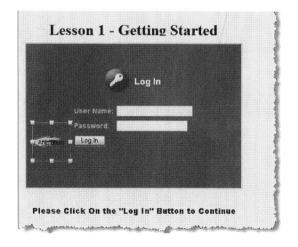

Text Animations

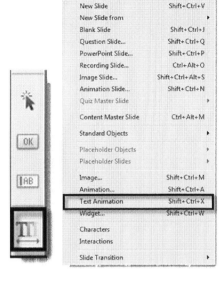

1. To insert a **Text Animation**: On the **Object Toolbar**, Click the **Insert Text Animation** tool.

Or, from the **Insert** menu: Click: **Text Animation**

2. Type the **text** that you will animate. Choose **font** type, size and whether you will **loop** the animation.

3. From the property inspector, on the **General** panel, choose the **type of animation** from the **Effect** drop down menu. After choosing an animation, you are given a quick preview.

4. Import any **audio**

you would like to associate with your Text Animation, if desired.

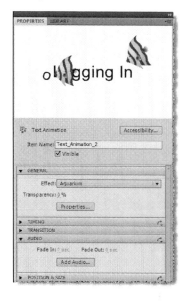

Effects

Object effects can help draw the user's attention to a particular section of a page. **Shadow and Reflection** are welcome new features in Captivate 7. It opens up a world of creative possibilities for developers. Effects can be divided into **four** broad categories, **Animation Effects** and **Filter Effects**, **Shadow and Reflection** and **Text Effects**. Text effects are handled in chapter 4 – "Adding Text Captions."

Pre-built Animation Effects

1. To insert an **Animation Effect** to an object, first select it. In this case, we are going to animate the Charts widget.

2. Launch the **Effects** panel by clicking: **Window / Effects**

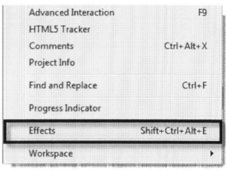

3. Click the **fx** icon at the bottom of the **Effects** panel and choose the effect you wish to add to the selected object.

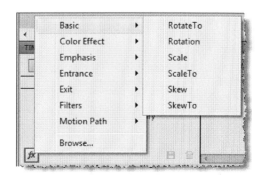

114

4. Adjust the timing of the effect.

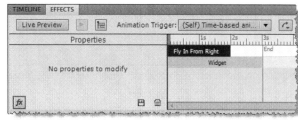

5. Click **Live Preview** to get a quick preview of the effect.

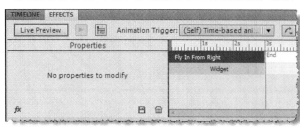

Importing Animation Effects – XML

In Flash, you can save tweens and other effects as XML files, and then import the XML files in Adobe Captivate 7. This method gives developers more flexibility and variety in the kinds of animation effects they can use in Captivate 7.

1. To insert an **Animation Effect** using XML, Click the **fx** icon at the bottom of the **Effects** panel and choose **Browse** to locate your XML file.

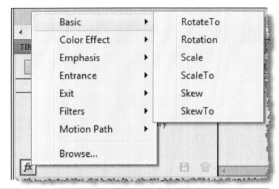

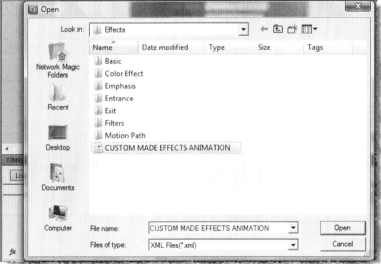

2. Click **Open**

3. Adjust the timing of the effect on the timeline.

Triggering Animation Effects

An interesting new feature in Captivate 7 is that you can trigger an effect to an object after a button is clicked or some other event. So for example, you can have an object rotate after the user clicks a button or a certain section of the screen.

1. To insert an **Animation Effect** to an object triggered by an **action**, first select the object. In this case, we are going to animate the Charts widget after clicking on a button.

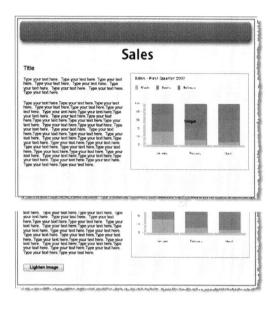

2. Add a button or click box to trigger the effect. We added a **text button**.

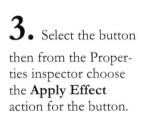

3. Select the button then from the Properties inspector choose the **Apply Effect** action for the button.

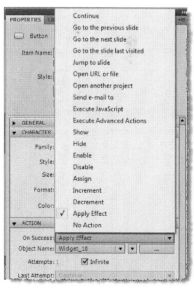

4. From the **Object Name** drop down menu, select the object to which the effect will be applied.

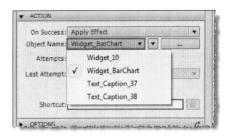

5. From the second drop down menu next to Object Name, de-select **Continue Playing the Project**, if you want to continually repeat the effect when the button is clicked.

6. Click the **Animation Palette**, to access the animation effects.

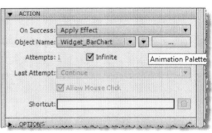

7. You are taken to the **fx** tab. Click the **fx** icon and choose an effect. We have chosen the **Set Brightness** effect.

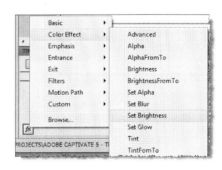

8. Adjust the **Properties** and timing of the effect.

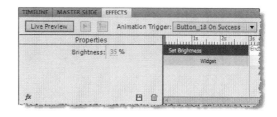

9. Chart **before** button is pressed.

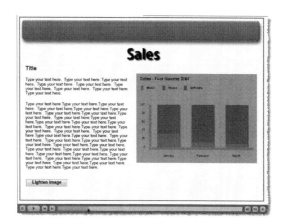

10. Chart **after** button is pressed.

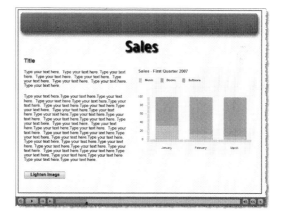

Filter Effects

Filter effects make graphics and text more visually appealing.

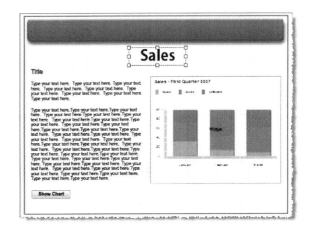

1. To insert a **Filter Effect** to an object, first select the object. In this case, we are going to add a **drop shadow** to the title "Sales."

2. Ensure that the Effects panel is opened by clicking **Window / Effects**. Click the **fx** icon at the bottom of the **Effects** panel and choose from the **Filters**:

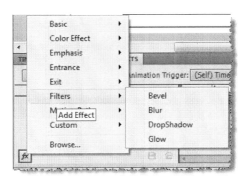

- *Bevel*
- *Blur*
- *Drop Shadow*
- *Glow*

3. Adjust the **Properties** and timing of the Filter effect. Increasing the amount of **Blur** on the X and Y axes, increases how dispersed is the drop shadow effect. Varying the **Strength** value determines the darkness or lightness of the effect.

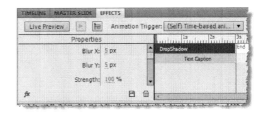

4. The drop **shadow** to the title "Sales" at run time.

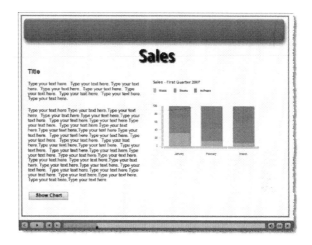

Shadow and Reflection

1. To add a drop **shadow** or **reflection** to an object, first select the object by clicking it.

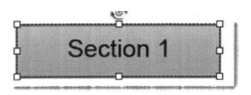

2. In the Property Inspector, expand the **Shadow and Reflection** accordion; place a **checkmark** in the Shadow checkbox. In the **Direction** dropdown menu for Shadow, choose either **Outer** or **Inner**. Outer

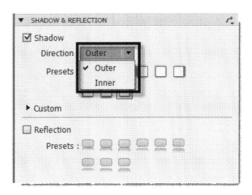

3. Choose one of the shadow **Presets** or create a **Custom** shadow by manipulating the values for **Blur**, **Angle**, **Color** and **Distance**.

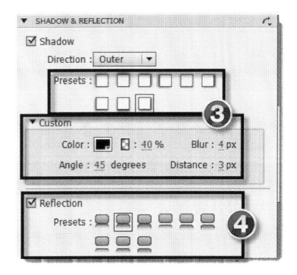

4. To add a Reflection, with the object selected, place a **checkmark** in the **Reflection** checkbox and select one of the available Presets.

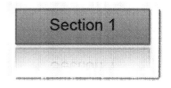

Smart Shapes

Smart Shapes are a new feature in Captivate 7. They are similar to the shapes you find in PowerPoint and you can use them to draw the user's attention to sections in your content. The ability to add text to Smart Shapes presents creative possibilities for presenting information instead of a text-only format. They are great for designing layouts in master slides.

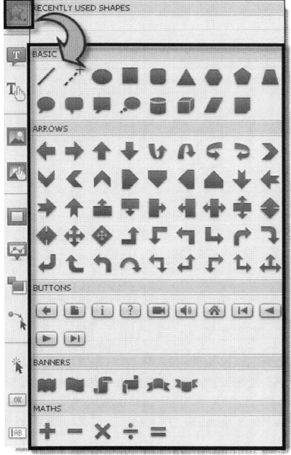

To learn more about using Smart Shapes, see Chapter 5 – "Adding Visuals."

8 - Adding Audio

Importing Audio

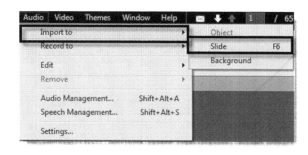

1. To insert audio into a slide, click

Audio > Import to > Slide.

2. Navigate to where your audio file is located. You can also use from a wide variety of audio clips from **Captivate's gallery**. Go to: Program Files /Adobe/Adobe Captivate 7/Gallery/Sound.

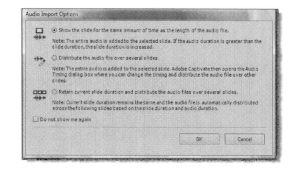

3. Select the split options for the audio. The first option should be chosen if you don't want the audio split among several slides.

4. You can **edit the audio** in a slide by **right clicking** over the audio in the timeline and selecting **edit** from the pop-up menu.

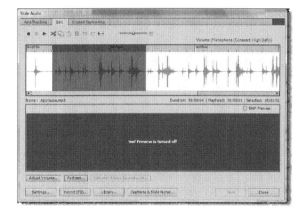

5. In the **Edit Audio** window, you can insert gaps of **silence** into the audio. You can also **trim**, **cut** and adjust the **volume** of the audio or sections of the audio file.

Adding Closed Captions for the Hearing Impaired

Adding closed captions in your learning modules is significant for accommodating learners with hearing disabilities. If closed captions are configured in the content of your courses, a learner can simply turn them on by clicking the closed caption button in the Captivate interface. They will then be presented with the text equivalent of all narration in the lessons. Adding closed captions for all audio files of recorded speech is one of the requirements for achieving 508 compliance.

1. In To add closed captions to a slide; first ensure that the Slide Notes panel is open by clicking:

Window > Slide Notes.

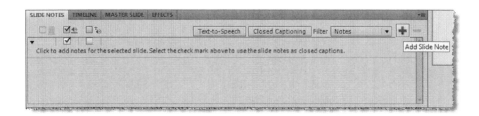

2. To add closed captions, click the **(+)** sign and simply type the notes in the **Slide Notes** panel and place a **check mark** under the **Audio CC** box in the **Slide Notes** panel.

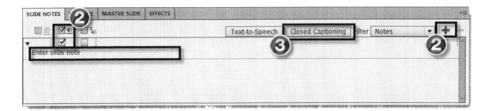

3. To edit the closed captions **font**, click the **Closed Captioning** button in the **Slide Notes** panel.

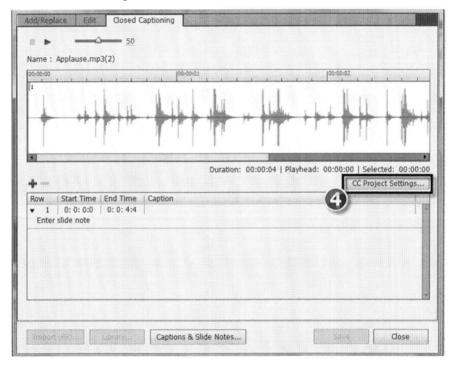

4. Click the **(+)** icon to add Markers and synchronize captions with the audio. Click the **CC Project Settings** button in Closed Captioning window that launches.

5. The **CC Project**
Settings window launches.

Choose your **Family** and
Size of **Font**.

Adding Audio Using Text-to-Speech

You can use the text-to-speech function to convert slide notes into narration. It's a cheaper alternative to hiring voice-over talent and a quick solution if you don't have facilities, access or resources for a recording studio. You need to download the text-to-speech voices for Captivate from the Adobe site. Neospeech and Loquendo voices are provided with your purchase of the software. Captivate 7 will load all voices installed in your system in addition to the ones shipped with the software.

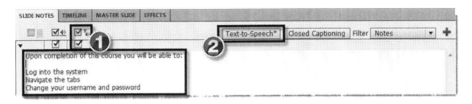

1. To add audio via the Text-to-speech feature, simply type the notes in the **Slide Notes** panel and place a **check mark** in the "**TTS**" box.

2. Click on the "**Text-to-Speech**" icon.

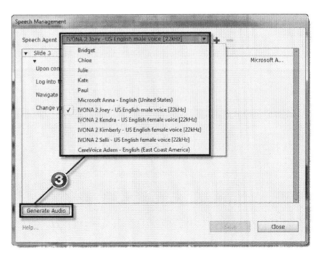

3. Choose one of the **TTS voices**: Kate, Paul or one of your installed voices and click **Generate Audio**.

4. The text is converted to speech based on the voice chosen.

5. Captivate adds the audio file for your converted text.

To ensure the highest audio quality without bloating the Captivate file size, your audio settings should be set at no lower than 96 kbps. Music sold on the Internet is usually encoded at 128 kbps or higher, which is near CD quality. It's also best to do the recordings outside of Captivate, and then import them afterwards.

Software such as Adobe Audition, Sony Sound Forge, Acondigital Acoustica or the free Audacity can produce excellent quality recordings. Choice of a microphone is also critical for high audio quality. I highly recommend a vocal condenser microphone or a professional headset with USB microphone that plugs directly into a laptop.

Play and Stop Audio Action

You can now add a **Play Audio** and **Stop Triggered Audio** action to any object in Captivate 7. This is a new feature and was not possible in previous versions of Captivate. You can have your user for example, click a button to hear a podcast or an audio presentation and then click a button to stop it.

1. To add the Play Audio action to an object, first select the object by clicking it.

2. In the Property Inspector, expand the Action accordion and choose **Play Audio**.

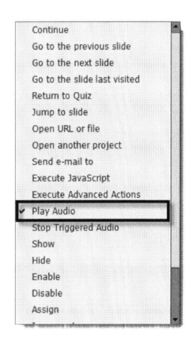

3. Click the **Browse** icon to locate the audio file.

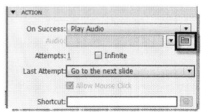

4. Navigate to where your audio file is located and select it.

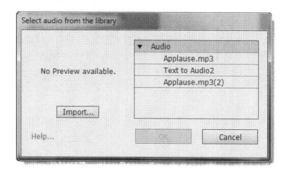

5. Specify the other settings for the audio file like **Attempts**, the action to be performed on **Last Attempt** of playing the audio file.

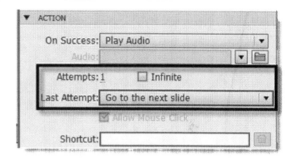

6. Repeat the above steps for the Stop Triggered Audio action, choosing **Stop Triggered Audio** in Step 2.

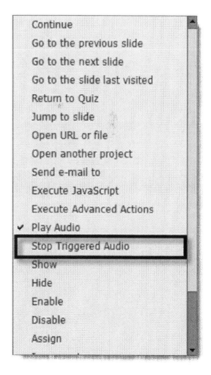

9 - Adding Video

1. To insert video into a slide, click

Video > Insert Slide Video.

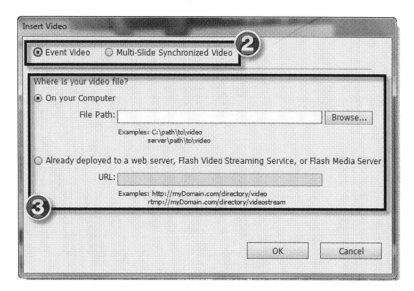

2. In the **Insert Video** dialog box that pops up, choose your Video Import options. **Event Video** plays on one slide. **Multi-Slide Video** plays across more than one slide.

3. Choose where your file located, either **On your computer** or **online**. If on your computer, navigate to where the file is located and select it. Captivate 7 will accept video files with extensions; **flv**, **f4v**, **avi**, **mp4**, **mov**, and **3gp**. If online, provide the **URL**.

In this example, we will navigate to a file on the computer.

4. Click **Open**, after locating and selecting your video.

5. Select in which folder you want **AME** to place the converted video. Click **Change Path** to place the video in a place other than the default setting.

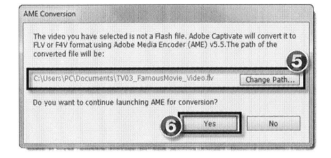

6. Click **Yes**, to allow **Adobe Media Encoder** (**AME**) to convert your video if it is not in a FLV format.

7. The conversion process in operation. This can take an extended time depending on the size of the video file.

8. The video
conversion process
completed.

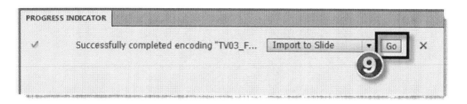

9. After completion of the video conversion, Under the **Progress
Indicator** tab in Captivate 7, with **Import to Slide** option selected click **Go.**

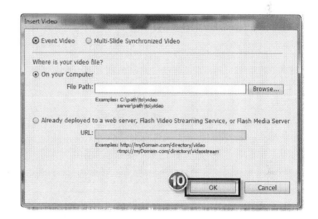

10. Click **OK**.

11. Launch the video
management tool to have more
control of videos in the project.
Click

Video / Video Management.

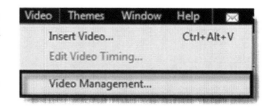

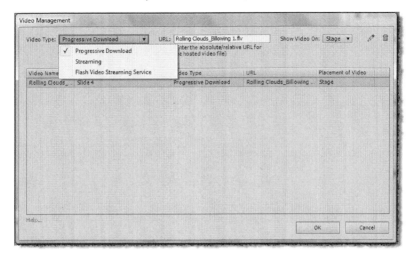

12. Using the Video Management tool, you can control how the video plays, and have a visual display of videos used in the project.

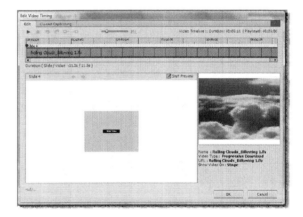

13. Click the **Edit Session** button to launch the **Edit Timing** window.

10 - Keeping the Project Organized, Synchronized and Standardized

Naming Conventions and Version Tracking

Huge Captivate projects with several developers and designers working on the same project can quickly become chaotic without established consensus for naming files and tracking different versions of a module. Often modules would be edited and revisions made based on feedback from the client or customer. These constant revisions need to be saved as separate files following file naming convention established by the team.

In general, it is good practice to name Captivate files with

- All lower case letters
- No spaces between words. Use the underscore for space
- Include a number at the end of the file name that indicates version number.

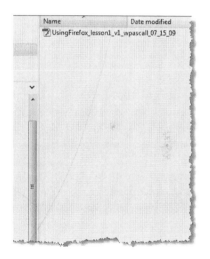

Locking Slides and Objects

Locking slides and specific objects in the timeline help prevent accidentally messing up elements that you have already built. This is a very good practice and will save you the agony of accidentally changing objects you have already configured and hours of rework. Locking objects in the timeline is especially helpful when you are working on objects that are in close proximity to each other or that may overlap each other on the screen.

1. To lock a slide, right click on any slide and choose **Lock Slide**.

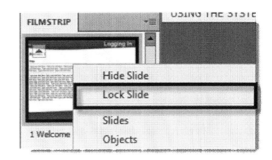

2. The slide is now **locked**. Nothing on this slide can be edited until you unlock the slide.

To unlock the slide right click on it and select **Unlock Slide** or simply click on the lock icon again.

3. To lock individual objects, simply click the **lock icon** for the object in the timeline.

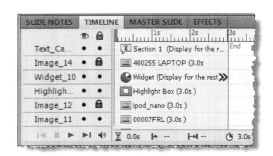

Labeling Slides

Labeling slides quickly becomes very important as your Captivate project grows in size. The more slides in the project, the more critical it is to place a label on each slide based on its content. Imagine the frustration of sifting through 200 slides in a Captivate module to make an edit, not knowing exactly where to find what you are looking for. Labeling slides aids both the client and developers to conduct quicker quality reviews and edits.

While each title in a Table of Contents (TOC) can be edited, labeling slides is also helpful for navigation since the TOC by default, uses the slide labels.

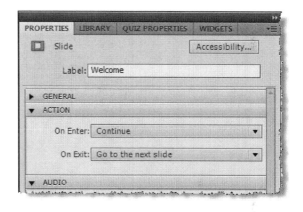

1. To label a slide, select the slide and type a desired name in the **Label** field of the **Properties** tab.

2. The label appears on the slide, making it easy to identify.

141

Grouping Slides

Grouping slides is a new feature in Captivate 7 and is very useful for keeping a project with many slides organized. Grouped slides can also be displayed in the table of contents. The group with its own name or topic can be expanded in the TOC to display sub-topics.

1. To group slides together, first select the slides, then right click and choose

Group / Create.

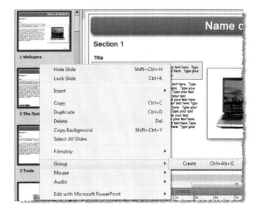

2. Type a desired name for the group in the **Label** field of the **Properties** tab.

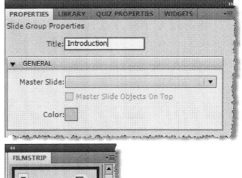

3. The name for the group is now displayed in the filmstrip. The group can be expanded and collapsed.

4. The grouped slides are also displayed in the **table of contents**. This project has 2 grouped slides: **Introduction** and **Metrics**.

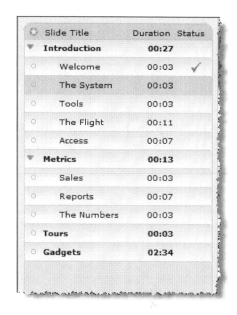

Grouping Objects

Captivate 7 has a new feature that allows developers to **group** a number of objects together into one object. Grouped objects can also be **Ungrouped**. This feature is great for complex work with objects and facilitates moving a bunch of objects together and also locking the design of several objects to prevent accidentally moving something out of place.

1. To group objects together, first select all the objects that need to be grouped, **right-click** and choose **Group**.

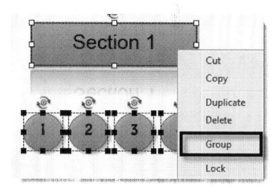

2. In the Property Inspector, Captivate 7 will give the group a unique name. You can change this name if desired. These objects can now be dragged around the stage as a group.

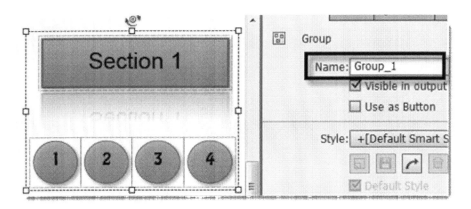

3. To ungroup objects that have been grouped, first select the grouped object, **right-click** and choose **Ungroup**.

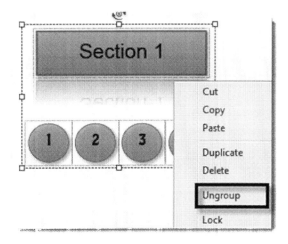

Timeline Synchronization

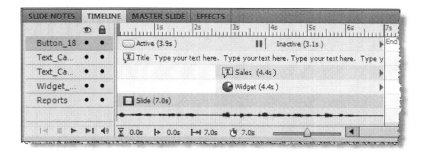

Objects can be aligned and moved to desired positions in the timeline. Slides with audio should be checked to ensure that the timing of the audio is synchronized with other objects on the slide such text and animations.

Keeping Things Consistent With Templates, Object Styles and Master Slides

As mentioned in chapter two, Captivate 7 offers some exciting tools for keeping a consistent look in your Captivate project. The combination of **themes, master slides, object styles** and **placeholders** in a template file provide more powerful tools for achieving consistency than previous versions of Captivate. If all developers and designers in a project build content using the same template, a high degree of consistency is achieved. This is critical for huge projects with several developers and designers working on different modules of a course. Please see **Chapter 2 - Themes, Preferences, Object Styles & Master Slides** for more information on using master slides, object styles and templates.

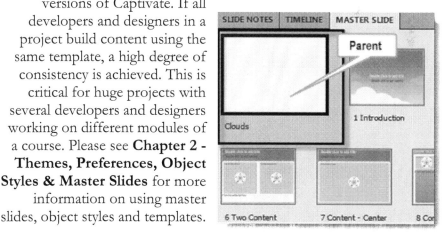

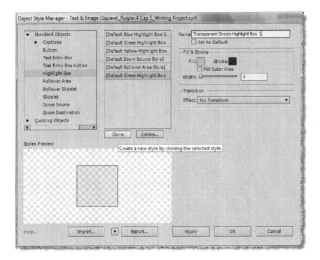

Object Style Manager

Alignment Tools for Consistency

Using the alignment tools in Captivate you can achieve consistency by having text and graphics all aligned exactly left, right, top or bottom and distributed evenly.

1. Ensure the **Alignment Toolbar** is visible by clicking:

Window / Align.

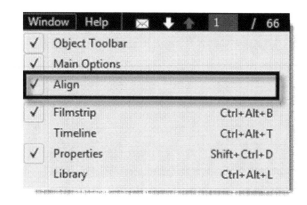

2. The **Alignment Toolbar** appears.

3. Objects **before** using alignment tools.

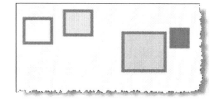

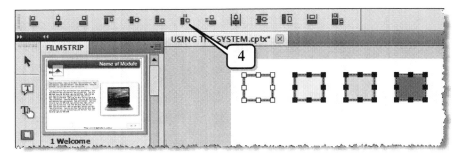

4. Objects become same width and evenly spaced horizontally after clicking: **Distribute Horizontally** and **Resize to Same Width.**

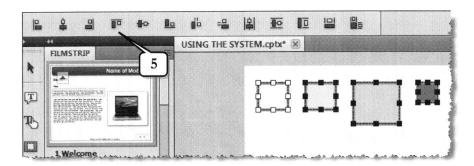

5. Objects become aligned evenly to the top after clicking **Align Top.**

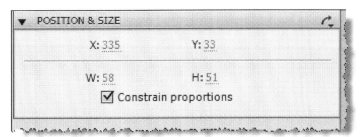

6. You can also use the coordinate numbers: X Axis (**X**) and Y Axis (**Y**) Width (**W**) and Height (**H**) to provide consistency in the dimensions and positions of objects. The objects pictured above, all have a (Y) coordinate value of 33. A (**Y**) coordinate value determines the **vertical** position of an object and the (**X**) value the **horizontal**.

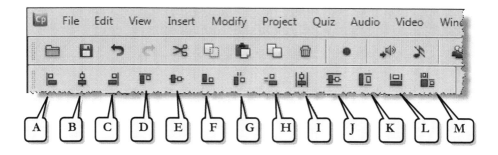

7. Using the **Align Toolbar**

A. Align Left
B. Align Center
C. Align Right
D. Align Top
E. Align Middle
F. Align Bottom
G. Distribute Horizontally
H. Distribute Vertically
I. Center Horizontally on the Slide/Slidelet
J. Center Vertically on the Slide/Slidelet
K. Resize to the same height
L. Resize to the same width
M. Resize to the same size

11 - Working with PowerPoint Projects

Creative Possibilities

Captivate 7 allows you not only to import PowerPoint presentations but also to edit those presentations inside Captivate. Using this workflow, you can combine the design advantages of PowerPoint with the interactive capabilities of Captivate. Although Captivate 7. I am happy to see that Captivate 7 has adopted some of the visually appealing design features that are present in PowerPoint. So now right in Captivate, you can design visually appealing Charts, diagrams, illustrations with gradients and drop shadows, reflections in combination with Smart Shapes and group objects together. Yet, a workflow of developing source documents in PowerPoint then importing them into Captivate for the finishing touches is possible.

Importing, Resizing and Editing

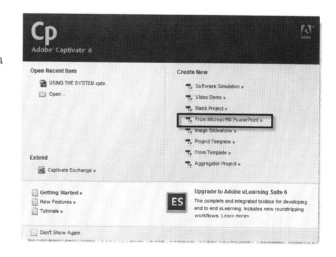

1. You can begin a PowerPoint project in Captivate by clicking **From Microsoft Power-Point** under the **Create New** menu of the **welcome screen**.

2. You can also import PowerPoint slides at any time during a Captivate project by clicking on:

Insert / PowerPoint Slide.

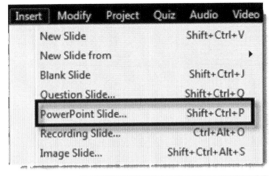

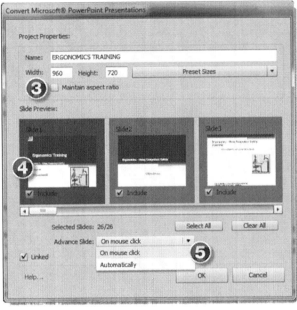

3. Choose the project size.

4. Choose the slides to be imported.

5. Choose how the slides should advance.

6. The imported PowerPoint slides appear in Captivate.

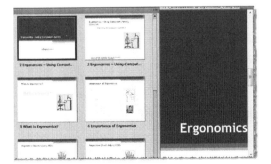

7. PowerPoint presentations imported into Captivate 7 can be edited inside Captivate by right-clicking on the imported PowerPoint slide and selecting one of the options from **Edit with Microsoft PowerPoint.**

8. You can also edit PowerPoint presentations from inside Captivate 7 by selecting the presentation inside **the library panel** and clicking the **Edit** icon.

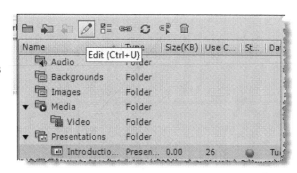

9. Save any changes to the PowerPoint presentation by clicking the **Save** button. Then click the close button. All changes are then reflected in the original PowerPoint file as well as the PowerPoint presentation embedded inside Captivate.

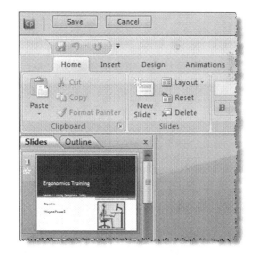

12 – Adding Interface, TOC and Skins

Skin Editor and Table of Contents

1. To add a skin and Table of Contents (TOC) to your Captivate project click:

Project / Skin Editor.

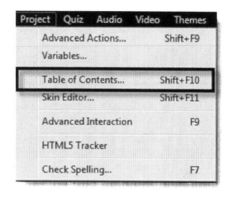

2. Click the **Playback Control icon**; choose your desired style, position, layout and colors for the **Playbar.**

3. Click the **Borders icon** and check **Show Borders** if needed and choose style of border.

Checking Show Borders will produce another SWF file for the border. Do NOT check this option if you want just ONE SWF file when you publish from Captivate.

4. Click the **TOC** icon and choose your style of **Skin**. Check **Show TOC** if you need a Table of Contents. The Table of Contents will then pull names from the labels on the slides. Each Name in the TOC can be edited by double clicking on it.

You can choose to have names in the TOC that are different than the slide labels.

.

5. Clicking the **Settings** button launches the **Skin TOC settings** dialog box. Here you can configure the **style, colors, transparency, fonts and Run Time Options** of the Table of Contents.

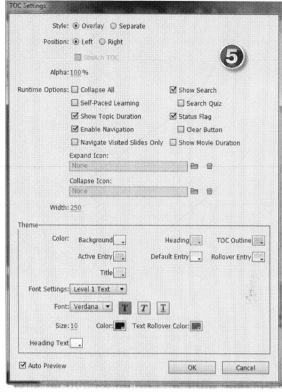

6. Clicking the **Info** button launches the **TOC Information** dialog box. Here you can insert information and a photo that will appear in the Table of Contents. Clicking the **Project Info** button will quickly copy Project Information, if supplied earlier, into the TOC Information box.

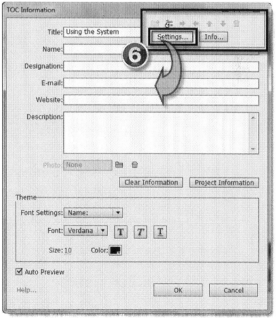

7. The Table of Contents appears at Run Time.

.

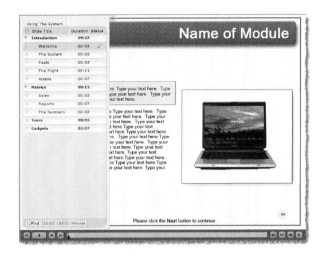

Aggregator Projects

The Aggregator feature allows developers to build an aggregated project consisting of several different flash files exported from Captivate 7. Using the Aggregator feature, you can build a course aggregated from multiple lessons, each represented by a published SWF file. The Aggregator also allows you to build a Table of Contents.

All the SWF files, however, must be exported from Captivate 7 and be the same ActionScript version, for the Aggregator feature to work. You cannot combine SWF files built in earlier versions of Captivate, and you cannot combine ActionScript 2 SWFs with ActionScript 3 SWFs. Remember that Captivate 7 uses ActionScript 3 programming.

Please note that while this is a convenient feature for small projects, it is not a practical solution for very large SWF files and will result very slow loading of the courses. For example, a course aggregated in Captivate from 12 SWF files, each consisting of 150-200 slides will result in a published SWF file from the Aggregator that is too huge for the course to run smoothly.

1. To begin an Aggregator project, click on **Aggregator Project** under the **Create New** menu in the welcome screen.

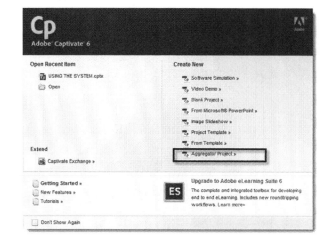

2. You can also begin an Aggregator project by clicking **File > New Project >Aggregator Project**.

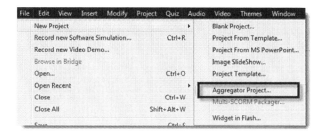

3. Click the **Add Module** icon (+).

4. Locate and select your SWF files exported from Captivate. Repeat steps 3 and 4 to add more SWF files to the Aggregator project.

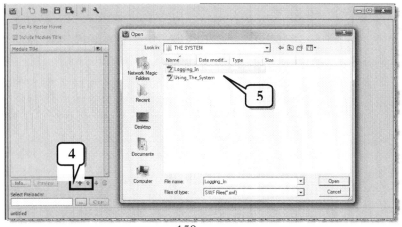

5. Choose the order of the modules by clicking the up and down arrows.

6. Select a SWF file which will be the master and select, **Set As Master Movie**. The TOC settings of this movie will then be applied to the others.

7. Save the Aggregator project.

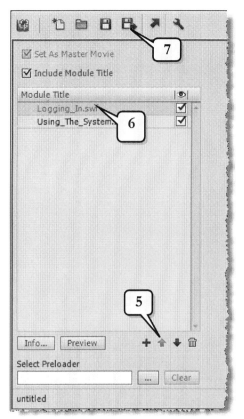

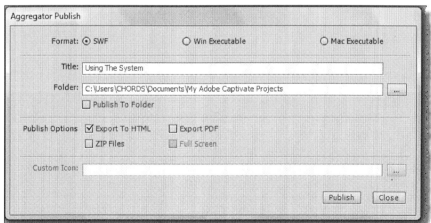

8. Publish the Aggregator project as either a Flash file or a Standalone (exe).

13 - Creating Quizzes

Defining Quiz Settings

1. Before adding a quiz, you need to establish the Quiz Preferences. Click **Quiz > Quiz Preferences** to begin.

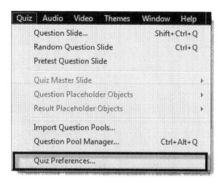

2. In the **Reporting** section under **Quiz**, set your preferences for reporting. This section is very important if you have a Learning Management System (LMS) and want quiz scores to be reported and tracked.

You can choose whether or not you want the quiz to be graded, what kind of interactions will be scored, whether or not you want grades reported and tracked on a LMS, format of the report, how the grades should be reported and settings for SCORM compliance. See **Chapter 14 - "Creating LMS-ready Files with SCORM Compliance"** for more information.

3. In the **Settings** section choose whether or not the quiz is **optional** or **required**. Choose from:

- **Optional** – the user can skip this quiz (Good for level 1 Assessment)
- **Required** – the user must take the quiz to continue (Recommended for level 2 assessment)
- **Pass required** – the user must pass the quiz to continue
- **Answer all** – the user must answer every question to continue

4. Choose Settings for:

Shuffle Answers, Show progress, Allow backward movement, Show score at end of quiz, Allow user to review quiz

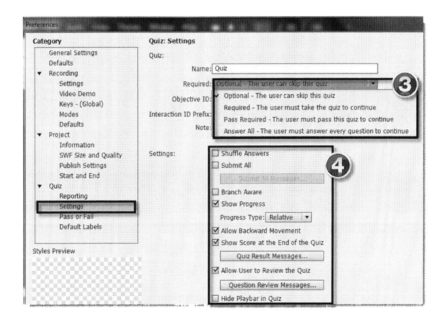

5. Clicking the **Quiz Result Messages** button on the **Settings** menu of the **Preferences** dialog box, launches the **Quiz Result Messages** dialog box.

Here you configure what messages are displayed after the user completes the quiz. You can customize your own **Pass Message, Fail Message and Email button text.**

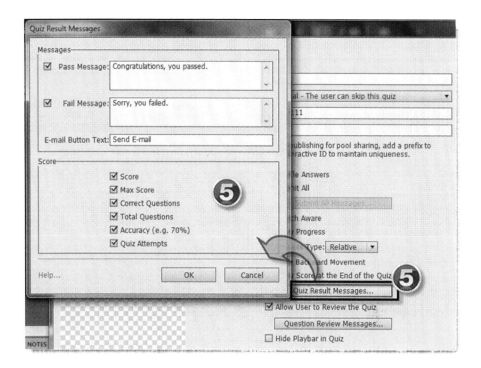

6. Clicking the **Quiz Review Messages** button on the **Settings** menu of the **Preferences** dialog box, launches the **Quiz Review Messages** dialog box.

Here you configure what messages are displayed after the user reviews the quiz upon completion. You can customize your own **Correct Message, Incomplete Message and Incorrect Message.**

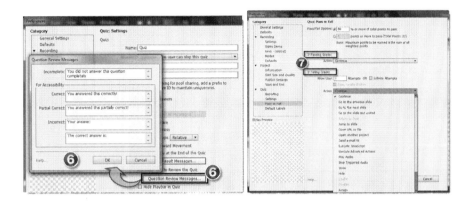

7. In the **Pass or Fail** section under **Quiz**, set your preferences for the passing grade. In this section you can also configure what **action** takes place if a user passes or fails. E.g. You can configure the actions that either sends an email to you with the passing grade, if the user passes or to send the student back to slide 1 to re-take the lessons if they fail. Set actions from the available list in the drop down menus for **If Passing Grade** and **If Failing Grade**.

Available Actions for Passing and Failing Grade:

Continue
The user is taken to the next defined action after clicking button.
Go To Previous Slide The user is taken to the previous slide after clicking button.
Go To Next Slide The user is taken to the next slide after clicking button.
Go To Last Visited Slide
The user is taken to the previously viewed slide after clicking button.
Return to Quiz
The user is taken back to the last attempted question if it was answered incorrectly.
Jump To Slide The user is taken to the specified slide after clicking button.
Open URL Or File
After clicking button, the user is taken to a website or file which opens.
Open another project
After clicking button, the user is taken to the specified Adobe Captivate project.
Send e-mail To
After clicking button, the user is taken to the default e-mail editor, which opens with an e-mail draft, addressed to the recipient as specified.
Execute JavaScript
After the user clicks button, Adobe Captivate executes the specified JavaScript.
Execute Shared Action (New), re-uses a shared Advanced Action
Execute Advanced Actions
After the user clicks button, Adobe Captivate runs the specified script. This includes multiple actions that are performed in the order specified by the user.
Play Audio, A user-click triggers a specified audio file to play
Stop Triggered Audio
After the user clicks the last triggered audio file stops playing
Show
After the user clicks button, the specified hidden object is made visible.
Hide
After the user clicks button, the specified object becomes hidden.
Assign
After the user clicks button, the value of the specified variable is set inside the object.
Increment
After user clicks button, the value of the specified variable is increased accordingly.
Decrement
After user clicks button, the value of the specified variable is decreased accordingly.
Apply Effect
After the user performs an action, it triggers an effect associated with the object
No Action
When the user clicks button, nothing happens.

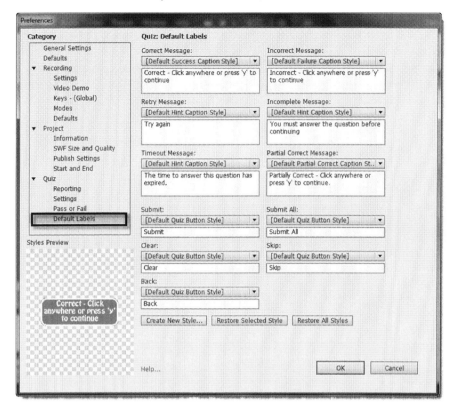

8. In the **Default Labels** section under **Quiz**, set your preferences for **question button labels** and **question feedback**.

9. You can also define styles for your question labels by clicking the **Create New Style** button.

Adding Questions

After setting the Question preferences, it's time to add some questions. Captivate 7 allows you to add nine types of questions to your quiz. A new feature not in previous versions of Captivate, is that you can simultaneously add more than one and multiple types of questions. Before adding questions, you need to plan how many and what types of questions, whether or not they will be graded, if they are just survey or "check your knowledge" questions. Here are the main types of questions you can add to a quiz:

Multiple Choice
The user selects one or more correct answers from a list.
True/False
The user chooses either True or False (or Yes or No).
Fill-In-The-Blank
The user completes the blank in a given statement.
Short Answer
The user supplies a short answer in the" form of a word or phrase.
Matching
The user matches words or phrases in two lists.
Hot Spot
The User is required to click on a certain spot on the screen.
Sequence
The user is required to arrange listed items in the correct sequence or order.
Rating Scale (Likert)
The user indicates their level of agreement to a given statement.
Random Question
The user is required to answer questions that are randomly selected from a question pool.

You can add a widget question slide only to question pools.

Remember that you can assess learners using other tools in Captivate besides the traditional quiz. You can, for example, have users complete information in text entry boxes as part of a guided simulation and have those interactions graded.

1. To add a question to your quiz, click:

Quiz > Question Slide.

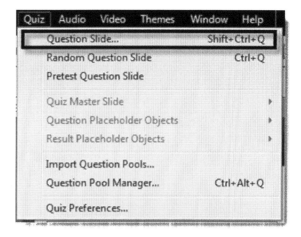

2. Choose the question types and quantity for each type of question. Then choose either **Graded Question**, **Survey Question** or **Pretest** for each.

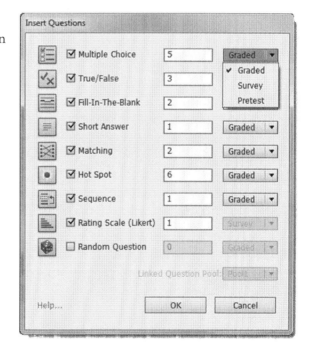

Pretest questions are a new feature in Captivate 7 that allow the user to be tested on a subject before attempting the questions. They are great for **"Check Your Knowledge"** type of questions.

3. Configure the correct answer by clicking the radio button that represents the correct response.

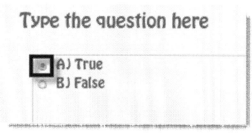

4. In the **Quiz Properties** tab, confirm whether it's a **Graded Survey or Pretest** Question from the **Type** drop down menu.

5. Specify the **Points, Penalty**, and **Numbering** of **Answers. Penalty** (New), deducts points if the user answers incorrectly.

6. Configure **options** for the answers including feedback **Captions** for when answers are

- Correct
- Incomplete
- Buttons

7. Configure **Actions** for the question:

- Number of Attempts
- Failure levels
- Action On Success

Preferences for this to occur.

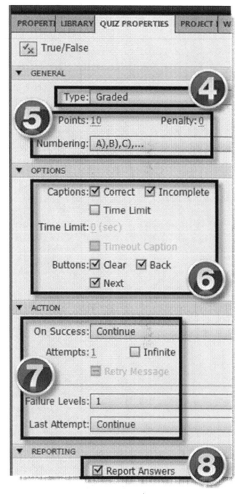

8. Check **Report Answers** if you want your quiz scores to be reported to a Learning Management System (LMS). You must also enable reporting in the Quiz Preferences for this to occur.

An alternative to adding questions in the traditional manner is to build and use a **Question Template**. As mentioned previously, using a template reduces development time and gives your project a consistent look, especially with many developers in a huge project. You can build your own question templates using the **Object Style Manager** to save styles for Quiz captions and buttons.

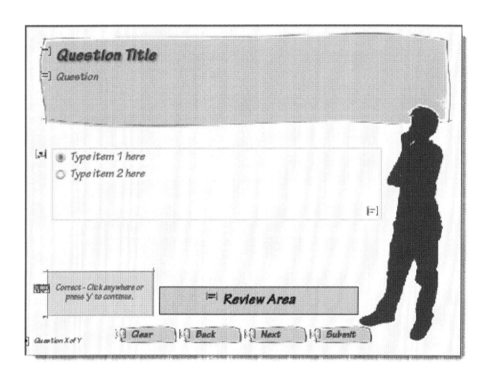

Adding Questions Using GIFT Format (New)

An alternative to adding questions in the traditional manner is using the **GIFT** (General Import Format Technology) format. This method is especially effective if you have large banks of questions and you want to save time and not to retype everything in Captivate. The GIFT file is in text format and is used extensively in Learning Management Systems like **Moodle**. The text file can be created in a simple text editor like Notepad. Here is a simple excerpt from a GIFT file:

```
// true/false
::Q1:: 1+1=2 {T}

// multiple choice with specified feedback for right and wrong answers
::Q2:: What's between orange and green in the spectrum?
{ =yellow # right; good! ~red # wrong, it's yellow ~blue # wrong, it's yellow }

// fill-in-the-blank
::Q3:: Two plus {=two =2} equals four.
```

1. To import questions in GIFT format into your project, click:

Quiz > Import Gift Format File

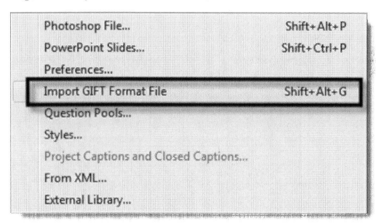

2. Select GIFT file and click **Open**.

14 - Creating LMS-ready Files with SCORM Compliance

What is SCORM and Its Benefits

A learning management system (LMS) is used to provide, track, and manage online training and education. The LMS makes it convenient for asynchronous learning, where students at any time can log into the system, take a desired or required course, get a score and that score is recorded and tracked in the LMS. Some popular Learning Management Systems are:

- Blackboard
- WebCT
- Plateau
- Saba
- Questionmark Perception

The files published from Captivate that you upload to the LMS should be compliant with the SCORM, AICC or PENS standards, depending on the requirements of the Learning Management System. **SCORM (Shareable Content Object Reference Model)** is a set of specifications and standards used to produce **reusable** e-learning objects. The aim of SCORM is to make content **shareable** among departments in a corporation, federal agencies and academic institutions. A reusable learning object represents a block of information and facilitates the use of that same information in several courses and modules. When SCORM is enabled in Captivate, each **published** package becomes a **SCO (Shareable Content Object)** with a SCO identifier in the accompanying published HTML file. The packed SCO is a **zipped file** with its contents being the published SWF file and associated HTML and JavaScript files. All SCOs can be uploaded to the LMS individually, or packaged into a single zipped file using the **SCORM Packager**. Learning Management Systems can communicate with and extract information from SCOs.

173

SCORM compliance, therefore, increases efficiency for information management and functioning of Learning Management Systems, decreases rework and decreases cost. SCORM is distributed by Advanced Distributed Learning, an organization under the US Department of Defense. AICC and PENs are similar eLearning standards but not as popular as SCORM as yet. AICC (Aviation Industry Computer-Based Training) is used mainly by the aviation industry and PENS (Package Exchange Notifications Services) facilitates automatic notification, transfer and delivery of content between Captivate and an LMS.

Fortunately, Captivate has the necessary tools to make eLearning modules SCORM compliant. After setting the required SCORM/AICC options in the **Quiz Settings** of Captivate, you complete the necessary information in the **Manifest** and publish. Captivate creates the necessary files encoded with information for compliance to these standards.

Benefits of SCORM
Sharing Reusable Learning Objects in an LMS

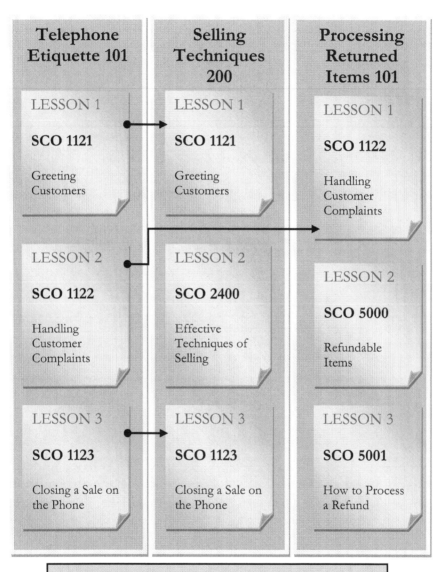

Telephone Etiquette 101	Selling Techniques 200	Processing Returned Items 101
LESSON 1	LESSON 1	LESSON 1
SCO 1121	SCO 1121	SCO 1122
Greeting Customers	Greeting Customers	Handling Customer Complaints
LESSON 2	LESSON 2	LESSON 2
SCO 1122	SCO 2400	SCO 5000
Handling Customer Complaints	Effective Techniques of Selling	Refundable Items
LESSON 3	LESSON 3	LESSON 3
SCO 1123	SCO 1123	SCO 5001
Closing a Sale on the Phone	Closing a Sale on the Phone	How to Process a Refund

SCORM (Shareable Content Object Reference Model)

SCORM (Shareable Content Object Reference Model) is all bout information management and efficiency by sharing and re-using information. Notice in the chart, the sharing of learning objects among three courses in a LMS. Each SCO was published from Captivate as a SCORM compliant lesson. When used in the manner outlined in the chart, this lesson becomes a reusable learning object. Notice that SCO 1122 which is lesson 2 under the course "Telephone Etiquette" is reused as lesson 1 under the course "Processing Returned Items." This is more efficient than having developers re-write the same information for the other courses that use it. It is easy to see how SCORM compliant courses can increase efficiency and reduce rework and reduce costs.

What is Tin Can and Its Benefits (New)

Captivate 7 has the capability to publish Tin Can compliant courses.

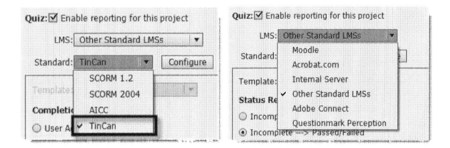

Tin Can is a new and growing set of standards for the eLearning industry that is superior to and may replace SCORM in the future. Tin Can compliant courses are not browser dependent and can track both online and offline user activity This makes it ideal for mobile learning. To publish for TinCan compliant LMSs, you need to select **Other Standard LMSs** in the reporting settings and specify **TinCan** in the Standard drop-down list.

Configuring Captivate to Publish SCORM Compliant Content to an LMS

The **Manifest** file created here will contain XML tags that describe the organization and structure of the project published to the LMS.

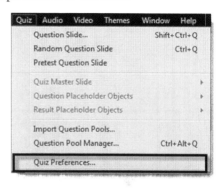

1. To begin configuring Captivate to publish SCORM compliant courses to a Learning Management System (LMS), click on

Quiz > Quiz Preferences.

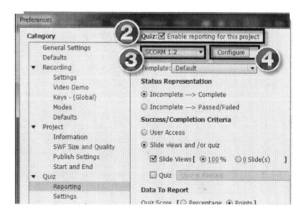

In the **Reporting** section under **Quiz**, set your preferences for reporting. This section is very important if you have a Learning Management System (LMS) and want scores of students to be reported and tracked.

2. Ensure **Enable Reporting for this Project** is selected then click on **Manifest.**

3. Choose the **SCORM Version** from the **Version** drop down list. The version chosen should be consistent with the requirements of your LMS. Most LMSs use SCORM 1.2.

4. Click Configure to configure the Manifest

5. Enter a name for the **Identifier**. This is the name used by the LMS to identify the manifest.

6. Enter a title into the **Title** area. This is what is viewed by students using the LMS.

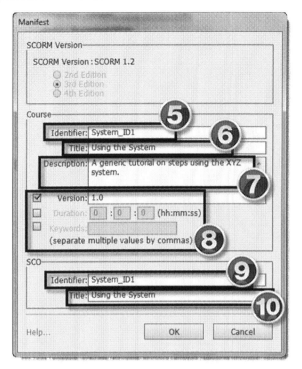

7. In the **Description** area, enter a short description about the lesson. This text will be displayed by the LMS in the course description.

8. Enter the **Version, Duration** and **Keywords** of the lesson. The **Version** differentiates the Manifest from others. If you are uploading the same project after modifying it, you should use a different version number. The **Duration** refers to how long it will take the user to complete the lesson. The **Keywords** let you enter keywords relevant to the lesson which become searchable in any Web page.

9. In the SCO / **Identifier** area, enter a name for the SCO. No spaces are allowed in a SCO Identifier.

10. In the SCO / **Title** area, enter the same title entered in the **Title** area under **Course.** Click **OK** to close the Manifest dialog

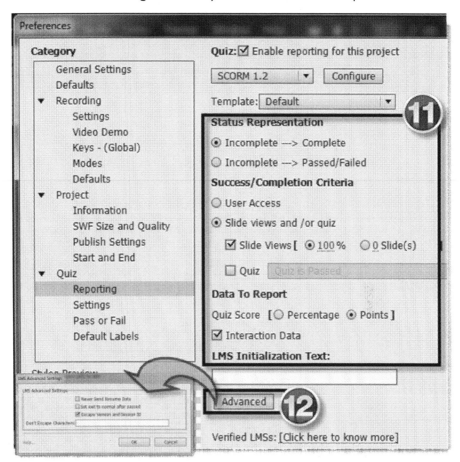

11. Complete the **Status Representation, Success/Completion Criteria** and **Data to Report** sections of Quiz Reporting to match the assessment needs determined by your organization.

12. Click **Advanced** to launch the **LMS Customization Settings** window.

Settings here govern how data is formatted and sent to the LMS.
Never Send Resume Data - Do NOT check
Escape Version and Session ID - Keep checked
Don't Escape Characters - Do not enter anything

What the LMS-ready Files Look Like

After configuring the quiz settings for SCORM compliance and reporting to an LMS, we must publish the project as a SWF file with an associate HTML file. Captivate then publishes other associated files along with the SWF and HTML files. If desired, all these files can be combined into a single file for convenience. When the Zip files output option is chosen, Captivate compresses, the entire set of published files into a single ZIP file, called a PIF (Package Interchange File).

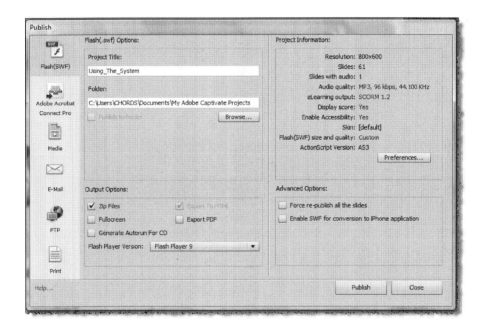

Though a PIF is not necessary for uploading SCORM compliant files to an LMS, it is always simpler to upload a single file to the LMS rather than many files. Each one of these zipped files represents a SCO in the LMS. Later we will see how several PIF s can be packaged together if desired, using a feature called the SCORM Packager.

Components of LMS-ready and SCORM Published Files. (Unzipped SCO)

1. **Cascading Style Sheet File (.css)**

A cascading style sheet to aid access by mobile users

2. **LMS supporting Files (.xsd)**

Contain information required by the LMS.

3. **Manifest File (imsmanifest.xml)**

This file is used to import the Adobe Captivate project into the LMS. The manifest file, **imsmanifest.xml**, contains the metadata of the project and its course structure.

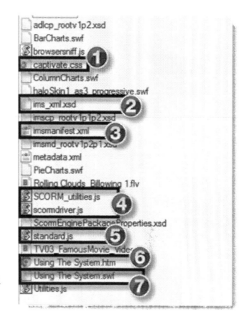

4. **SCORM JavaScript Files (.js)**

These files ensure compliance to the SCORM standards during run time.

5. **Standard JavaScript File (.js)**

Acts as a link between the SWF file and the LMS. Adobe Captivate sends tracking data to the LMS using the JavaScript APIs.

6. **HTML File (.htm)**

Launches the Adobe Captivate project from the LMS.

7. **SWF File (.swf)**

The flash file with the contents of the published project is stored in the SWF file.

15 - Publishing

Publishing Individual SCOs for an LMS

To begin publishing a SCORM compliant package ready for uploading to an LMS. Ensure that the SCORM/AICC options and quiz reporting options are enabled as described previously.

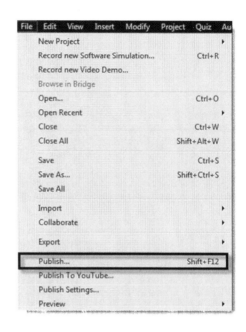

1. Click: **File > Publish.**

2. Select **SWF/HTML5** as the format.

3. Choose **Output Format Options.** If publishing for **PC** users ensure that **SWF** is checked. For users on **mobile devices**, ensure that **HTML5** is checked.

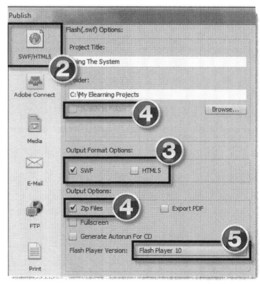

4. Select **Zip Files** if you are publishing for an **LMS.** This is the file you will upload to the LMS. If not, leave it unchecked and check **Publish to Folder.**

5. Choose your **Flash Player version.**

Multi-SCORM Packager Projects (New)

The **Multi-SCORM Packager** that was part of Captivate 5 and missing in Captivate 6 is now back in Captivate 7. It is used for combining several published SCOs into one packaged zipped file.

The SCORM Packager offers a quick way of uploading several published SCOs to an LMS. It does so by combining multiple published Captivate SCOs into one packaged, zipped file. The Packager creates a Table of Contents with the names of the different modules. This zipped file can then be uploaded to the LMS.

To access the Multi-SCORM Packager click:

File > New Project > Multi-SCORM Packager

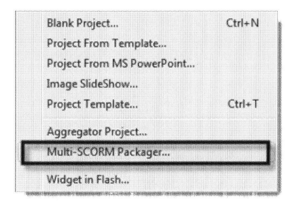

Publishing for an Autorun CD

Autorun CD for Windows and Mac

To have your Captivate project available as an autorun CD for Windows and Macintosh, you will need to publish your project as a Windows executable file (**exe**).or a Mac executable file (app).

1. Click: **File** > **Publish.**

2. Select **Media** as the format.

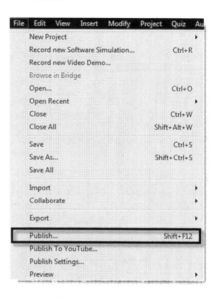

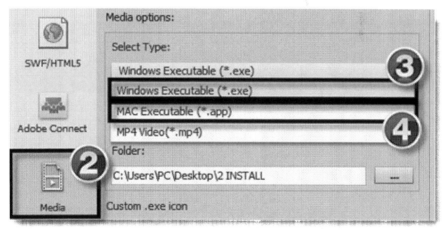

3. From the **Select Type** drop down menu, select **Windows Executable (*.exe)** for a PC.

4. Select **MAC Executable (*.app)** if you are preparing an autorun CD for a Macintosh system.

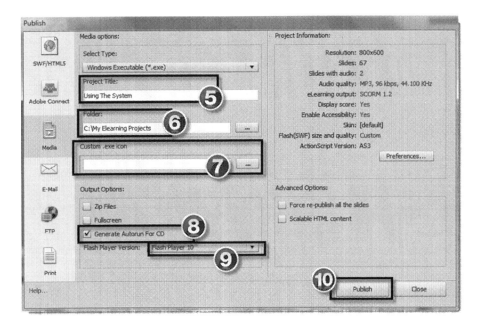

5. In the **Project Title** field, enter a name for the executable file.

6. In the **Folder** section, select the path leading to the folder where the file will be published.

7. In the **Custom.exe icon** section, select the icon that will represent the .exe file. You may need software that can produce icons, if you don't have an icon ready.

8. In the **Output Options,** select **Generate autorun for CD**. You can also select Zip files, which compresses the executable and all associated files into one zip file.

9. Choose your **Flash Player Version.**

10. Click **Publish.**

11. Use your CD burning software to burn all the **published files** to a CD or DVD.

Ensure that all files contained in the publish folder are added to the CD. Any externally linked files must be manually moved to the same folder where the executable file is published and also burned to the CD. Any SWF files added to the project that has other linked or dependent files, such as JavaScript, xml files etc., must also be manually moved into the publish folder and included in the CD. The .inf file is needed to launch the project automatically when the CD is inserted into the computer.

Publishing for the iPad

Publishing for users of mobile devices, specifically the iPad, is a great new feature in Captivate 7. To publish Captivate projects so that they run correctly on the iPad, you first need to use one of the iPad templates to begin the project.

1. Click: **File > New Project**

OR From the Welcome screen click **Blank Project.**

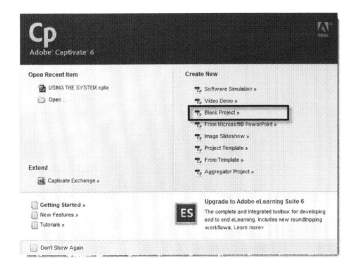

2. In the **New Blank Project** Window that launches, select one of the iPad Project Resolutions: **Apple iPad Landscape (1024 x 672)** or **Apple iPad Portrait (768 x 928)** and click **OK.**. Captivate will now scale and configure your project for playback on the iPad.

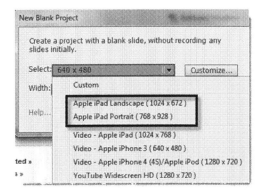

3. Develop and save your project. At this point you may also choose to design an **iPad template** by customizing one of the available Themes then save your work as a **.cptl** file.

4.

While developing, run the **HTML5 Tracker** (Project > HTML5 Tracker) occasionally to verify what is supported in HTML5 format and if there are any errors. Not all objects and interactions are supported on the iPad

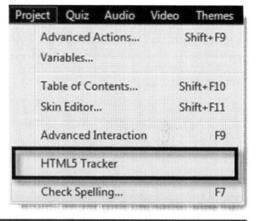

It is a great idea while working on iPad/Mobile projects to keep the **HTML5 Tracker** open at all times, so you can constantly monitor what objects and interactions are not supported in HTML 5 output. Click **Window > HTML5 Tracker** to have it opened as a tab.

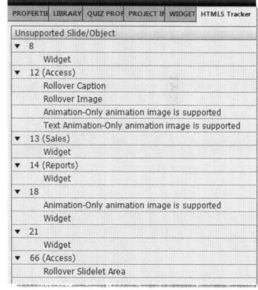

Unsupported Items in HTML5 Output

Adobe has documented that the following items are not supported in HTML5 output and may therefore encounter playback problems on the iPad. Refrain from using them for mLearning projects.

Not Supported:

- Text and SWF animations (only the first frame is visible).
- Mouse click animations (only one default click effect is supported).
- Question pools, Likert question slides, and random question slides (supported in Cp 7 and later).
- Slide transitions.
- Slide background if a SWF file is used.
- Audio attached to invisible objects.
- Mouse right-click and double-click.
- Borders (supported in Cp 7 and later).
- Reporting to internal server and Acrobat.com (supported in Cp 7 and later).
- Video streaming using RTMP is not supported in HTML5 output.
    - *Note: FLV files that are created using On2VP6 codec only are supported in the HTML5 output.*

5. When you are ready to publish, click **File** > **Publish**

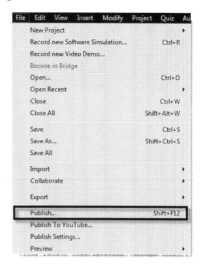

6. Select **SWF/HTML5** as the format.

7. Ensure that **HTML5** is checked.

8. Choose **Zip Files** for convenient uploading to an **LMS**.

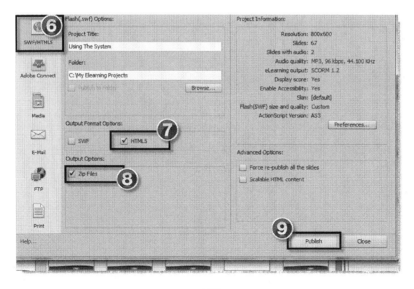

9. Click **Publish**

10. If there are

unsupported items in HTML5 output, you will receive a final warning in a pop-up window. Click **No** to correct those items or **Yes** to proceed. After uploading to the LMS, your course is ready for iPad users.

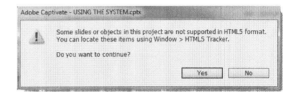

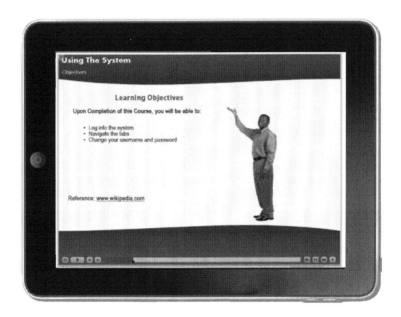

Publishing Apps for Mobile Devices (New)

The Adobe Captivate App Packager allows you to produce your projects as native iOS and Android applications. You can embed HTML5 animations for mobile devices using **Adobe Edge Connect** and you will need an **Adobe PhoneGap Build** service.

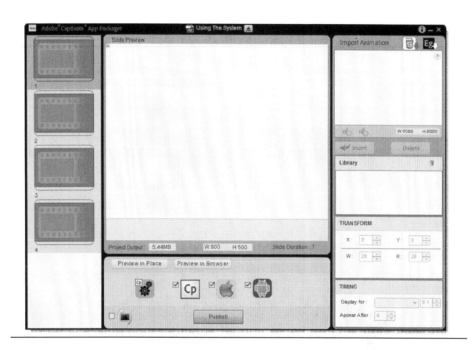

Once you have the additional Adobe Edge and Phone Gap services you can supplement the animations and interactions created by Captivate with extra polished ones using this tool.

Use the path below to access the **App Packager**:

Windows (7 & 8)
32-bit: C:\Program Files (x86) \Common Files\Adobe\Adobe Captivate App Packager
64-bit: C:\Program Files\Common Files\Adobe\Adobe Captivate App Packager

Mac: /Applications/Adobe/Adobe Captivate App Packager

About the Author

Wayne Pascall is an instructional technologist, artist, musician and author. Many of his creative works can be accessed on various sites on The Internet. He holds Bachelor's degrees in Human Resources and Psychology with a Master's in Instructional Technology. Wayne also uses his skills as a fine artist to design and prepare graphics for eLearning courses.

Other Titles by the Author:

Adobe Captivate 7 – Advanced Techniques (With Flash Integration)

Learn the **advanced features** of Captivate 7 by working through exercises in creative and advanced projects with clear step-by-step guidelines. These exercises are ideal for creative developers who would like to use Captivate beyond its normal uses or to add some flair to traditional projects.

ISBN - 978-1492847021

For more Captivate and eLearning products by the author, visit:

www.elearnvisual.com

Made in the USA
Charleston, SC
28 November 2013